STEWART LANSLEY

A SHARING ECONOMY

How social wealth funds can tackle inequality and balance the books

POLICY PRESS SHORTS INSIGHTS

First published in Great Britain in 2016 by

Policy Press
University of Bristol
1-9 Old Park Hill
Bristol
BS2 8BB
UK
t: +44 (0)117 954 5940
pp-info@bristol.ac.uk
www.policypress.co.uk

North America office:
Policy Press
c/o The University of Chicago Press
1427 East 60th Street
Chicago, IL 60637, USA
t: +1 773 702 7700
f: +1 773 702 9756
sales@press.uchicago.edu
www.press.uchicago.edu

British Library Cataloguing in Publication Data
A catalogue record for this book is available from the British Library.

Library of Congress Cataloging-in-Publication Data
A catalog record for this book has been requested.

ISBN 978 1 44733 143 8 (paperback)
ISBN 978 1 44733 145 2 (ePub)
ISBN 978 1 44733 146 9 (Mobi)

Cover design by Andrew Corbett
Front cover: image kindly supplied by istock
Printed and bound in Great Britain by CMP, Poole
Policy Press uses environmentally responsible print partners

Also by Stewart Lansley

Poverty and Progress in Britain (with GC Fiegehen and AD Smith)

Housing and Public Policy

Poor Britain (with Joanna Mack)

After the Gold Rush

Top Man: How Philip Green Built his High Street Empire (with Andy Forrester)

Rich Britain: The Rise and Rise of the Super-Wealthy

Londongrad: From Russia with Cash (with Mark Hollingsworth)

The Cost of Inequality

Breadline Britain: The Rise of Mass Poverty (with Joanna Mack)

Contents

About the author

Stewart Lansley is a visiting fellow at The Townsend Centre for International Poverty Research, University of Bristol. He has written widely on poverty, wealth and inequality. He is the co-author of *Breadline Britain: The Rise of Mass Poverty* (with Joanna Mack) and the author of *The Cost of Inequality* and of *Rich Britain*. He has held a variety of academic and journalistic positions and was an executive producer in the current affairs department of the BBC from 1998-2008.

Acknowledgements

Many friends and colleagues have helped with this book. A huge thanks in particular to Steve Schifferes who generously read an early draft and made a raft of immensely helpful and insightful comments. I am grateful too for very helpful comments on earlier chapters from – and for conversations about the ideas in the book with – Pat Conorty, Joe Cox, Neal Lawson, Joanna Mack, Anne Rannie, Derek Reed, Jon Shields, Malcolm Torry, David Webster and Stuart White. Thanks too for many discussions on these and related issues with Howard Reed. I would also like to thank two anonymous referees for helpful suggestions on an early proposal for the book, Compass for publishing an earlier think piece on the potential of social wealth funds, and for feedback from participants in seminars where some of the ideas have been aired. Finally, a special thank you to the Policy Press team for ensuring that all has gone remarkably smoothly. The royalties from the book will be donated to an anti-poverty charity.

Preface

The UK badly needs a change of course. Its economic model has proved unable to deliver a sustainable economic and social system. The economy, built around disproportionate power to the owners of capital, works well for some. But it has failed to meet a primary political goal: to ensure that *all* citizens participate in economic progress. It is failing too on another vital social aim – to guarantee a minimum acceptable standard of living for all. As a result, the UK is becoming an ever more polarised society, one marked by more extreme levels of wealth for the few, affluence for a minority but increasing insecurity and impoverishment for those left behind.

There is an urgent need to forge a new economic model, 'a sharing economy', one that shares prosperity and delivers greater security across the divide, economic and social. The idea of a 'sharing economy' has mostly been used in recent months to describe the potential of a developing 'peer-to-peer economy`, involving the greater sharing of private assets through bartering, leasing and the swapping of goods, time and expertise. Among the most quoted examples of such collaboration are the global rental website Airbnb, and the transport-sharing platform Uber.[1] Here the term is used in a more comprehensive way, to describe a new way of managing the economy to ensure that the proceeds of economic activity and of growing prosperity are shared more evenly across society. Building a more progressive political economy in which the cake is more evenly shared is not just desirable, it is an economic imperative. The current model of corporate capitalism, based on great private concentrations of capital and too heavily geared towards enriching the few at the expense of the many, is weakening the productive base and making the economy much more prone to crisis.

Creating a sharing economy will require a range of radical changes to the UK's model of capitalism. This book examines one possible route to change – the social wealth fund. Social wealth funds are a potentially powerful tool in the progressive policy armoury. They are collectively held financial funds, created from the pooling of resources, fully owned by the public and used for the benefit of society as a whole. They would ensure that a higher proportion of the national wealth is held in common and used for the public good and not to serve the interests of the few.

Though they have yet to be established in the UK, social wealth funds are not a new idea and history is rich with examples. In recent years, many countries have introduced such pooled funds, mainly by the creation of sovereign wealth funds. Most of these operate in a highly secretive way as little more than the investment wing of the state. The great majority are not used to promote wider social gains, and fall well short of how a model fund would work. Nevertheless, there are a number of examples, current and past, such as those operating in Norway and Alaska and the former wage-earner fund model operating in Sweden during the 1980s, that could be used as the basis for developing a progressive UK version.

A model social wealth fund would aim to mobilise resources from one or more areas, putting them to use for agreed economic and social goals. A primary source of funding would be from the better management of public assets. These assets, together worth an estimated £1.2 trillion and with significant commercial potential, should be brought together into a single ring-fenced fund to form a giant pool of commonly held wealth. This would preserve what remains of 'the family silver' – the nation's collectively owned assets built up over decades – and ensure that the revenue from higher returns and sales would be used to build the value of the pooled fund.

Funding could also come from other sources, including the public revenue from a range of natural resources, from the redirection of the proceeds of some existing taxation, or the establishment of new taxation and, most radically, from ways of diluting private capital ownership. The latter could include a new private levy on share ownership, or new charges on certain forms of financial and commercial transactions – such as merger and acquisition activity – that involve the unearned extraction of existing corporate wealth for a small commercial elite.

Such funds would be run in a fully transparent way, at arm's length from the state through broadly based independent boards. They would be allowed to grow over time, with part of the returns being reinvested and part being used to fund agreed social programmes. By building large pools of socially owned capital, social wealth funds would ensure that a higher proportion of the national wealth is owned socially, thus creating an important counter to the concentration of private capital and the strength of big business. If part of the finance were to come from new charges on some commercial activity, they would contribute to the dilution of today's great concentrations of capital, the primary source of growing inequality over recent decades.

Social wealth funds would embrace a set of economic and social values that are quite distinct from those implicit in the use of market forces, and could be used to ensure that more of the private unearned gains enjoyed by individuals are pooled and shared across society. Through greater transparency in public policy, such funds could prove popular with the public. They would, crucially, inject more medium- and long-term planning into areas of public and social policy that are too often the subject of political short-termism. They will take time to build but, when established, will provide robust long-term funding, while ensuring that the gains from commonly held wealth are shared by future generations as well as the current generation.

Social wealth funds have the potential to tackle a number of the deep-seated economic and social weaknesses in the current UK model. They could be used to raise the level of investment in infrastructure – an essential requirement for boosting the UK's low level of productivity growth – and boost the depleted level of social capital. They would also offer a degree of protection to public investment programmes during fiscal crises. They could help to fund measures that aided upward social mobility, encouraging a fairer spread of economic and social opportunities, and help to fill the growing gaps in key areas of public social provision. Together, such funds would help to ensure that key economic and social activities – from investment to social care – command a higher share of economic activity than has been the case in the past.

Imagine the shape of the British economy today if one or more of such funds had been created along these lines in the past. With billions invested in these funds over time, and parts of the fund used and part reinvested, they would have grown to represent a very sizeable chunk of the economy's overall wealth. Such collectivised funds would have enabled a much higher level of public investment, while creating a much better balance in the state of the public finances. If an established fund existed today, it would be able to relieve some of the economic and social pressures currently facing the UK.

Such funds might also be used to finance a direct payment to citizens through an annual citizen's dividend or, more radically, through a regular citizen's income. Social wealth funds and citizen's payments could operate as separate and independent elements of a new alternative economic model. However, since such funds would be owned by all citizens there is a logic to using part of their gain to fund payments to all individuals. Since 1982, the state of Alaska has used its sovereign wealth fund, financed by oil revenue, to fund just such a citizen's dividend. Alternatively, social wealth funds could be used to part-fund the cost of a citizen's income scheme. Such a scheme would constitute a regular weekly, unconditional income to all as a right of citizenship. A citizen's income scheme would be a universal system that would involve a profound revolution in the way we organise income support. It would enjoy many merits over the existing, increasingly means-tested and punitive, model of social security. In particular, it would offer much greater security, in what is becoming an increasingly fragile labour market.

The introduction of social wealth funds and/or a citizen's income scheme would not be without controversy. More radical schemes for funding a social wealth fund, such as a charge on shareholders, would no doubt provoke widespread business opposition, while the merits of payments to citizens will continue to be hotly debated. But ultimately both schemes would contribute to building a more robust economy and greater social security. It is surely time that both are much more widely debated.

Stewart Lansley
December 2015

ONE

'All-out assault': inequality and corporate capitalism

In the last few years, inequality has been rising up the national and global political agenda. World leaders have been tripping over themselves to declare verbal war on the rising income gap. 'Inequality is the root of social evil,' declared Pope Francis in 2014. It's 'the defining challenge of our time,' added President Obama.

In the UK, the church, leading charities and a diversity of political leaders have all launched attacks on the growing social and economic divide. They include leading Conservative politicians. Conservatives should be 'warriors for the dispossessed,' declared Cabinet Minister Michael Gove a few weeks before the 2015 election.[1] After the election, the Prime Minister, David Cameron, promised delegates to the Conservative Party Conference 'an all-out assault on poverty'.[2] Until the 2008 financial crash, the question of inequality barely registered on the political Richter scale. In power from 1997, New Labour dropped the question of the rising gap between top and bottom from their agenda, concentrating on ways to raise the income floor and ignoring the ever-growing personal fortunes being accumulated at the top.

The move towards a more equal society had been one of the most enduring of early post-war trends. Then from the mid-1970s, this equalising process first faltered and then went into reverse. While the rising share of national income taken by the top 1% is a trend that has been occurring in a majority of rich nations, it has been especially sharp in the UK and the United States. Once one of the most equal of rich nations, the UK is now near the top of the global inequality league.[3]

To date, the multiple voices of protest against rising inequality have yet to be translated into action. The mechanisms that allow a small, powerful business and financial elite to colonise the gains from growth remain largely in place. As a result, in the UK and across much of the globe, the richest 1% have continued to pull away from the rest through the post-crisis years.[4]

High levels of inequality are built into the Anglo-Saxon model of capitalism. What is at work, writes the influential French economist Thomas Piketty, is 'a fundamental force for divergence', a natural, inbuilt tendency to generate an ever-growing gap.[5] There are, of course, various models of capitalism at work across the globe today. There are significant differences, for example, between the dominant Anglo-Saxon, pro-inequality model operating in the UK and the US and the less market-oriented and more inclusive models at work in parts of continental Europe. Nevertheless, inequality levels have also been rising, if mildly, in some traditional egalitarian European states, though the income gap remains much higher in some nations than others. The critique in this book applies in the main to the market-based corporate model that operates in the UK, though its proposals could be applied much more widely.

This book argues that tackling inequality requires more than tinkering with this system, a modest hike in the minimum wage here, or tougher reforms on corporate governance there. Creating a more equal society requires a wholly different economic and social model, one aimed at building a new 'sharing economy', one which builds a basic floor below which nobody would fall, a lower ceiling at the top and which ensures that the fruits of economic activity are more evenly shared than in recent decades.

This may sound utopian. However, the need for fundamental reform of the UK's inequality driving economic model is now being increasingly acknowledged. Criticisms that once flowed only from left-of-centre commentators are now being echoed by a much wider range of influential opinion, from senior figures in the Bank of England to former advisers to the Conservative Party, not just because the model drives excessive levels of inequality, but because it also threatens economic viability.

But how do we ensure that the cake is more evenly divided? How can the economy be reformed so that it is both less unequal and more productive? Is it possible to translate the verbal war into effective change?

There are many possible strategies for reducing the yawning income gap. But effective and enduring change depends above all on challenging the disproportionate grip on power and wealth enjoyed by a tiny elite of business and corporate leaders and financiers. As Steve Hilton, strategist to David Cameron during the coalition years, put it bluntly in *The Observer* in July 2015: 'We need an all-out assault on the concentration of economic power that allows the exploitation of workers, customers, suppliers and wider society'. We must, he continued, stand up 'to the smug plutocrats raking in their millions while ripping off the rest of us.'[6]

There is now a live debate on the need for reform, on how to build a sharing economy, a more 'inclusive model' of capitalism. Mark Carney, the Governor of the Bank of England, has called for a new 'basic social contract comprised of relative equality of outcomes, equality of opportunity and fairness across the generations'.[7] Debate there may be. But there is little to show for it. The post-1980s model of capitalism at work in the UK and the US and a number of other countries may be under verbal attack, but it remains largely intact.

Because of this, the most likely trend is a continuing widening of the gap, in the UK and across nations. As the Paris-based club of rich nations, the Organisation for Economic Co-operation and Development (OECD), has predicted, 'With unchanged policies, the average OECD country will face an increase in (pre-tax) earnings inequality by 30% in 2060, facing almost the same level of inequality as is seen in the US today'.[8]

The UK is poorly placed to resist this trend. It has evolved an increasingly dysfunctional economic model, one that has not merely produced an increasingly skewed distribution of the cake but presided over a much weakened economic performance as well. At the heart of these problems is the overdominance of privately owned capital.

Critical to the way economies function is the relationship between three key elements: the workforce, capital and the state. Models of capitalism are defined by how power is dispersed across this triangle. If the workforce gets too powerful and grabs too big a share, capital – with a critical role in the overall level of wealth, jobs and growth – suffers. An overdominant capital, on the other hand, not only brings much higher levels of inbuilt poverty and inequality, but can simultaneously threaten economic progress.

The post-war era to the early 1970s brought a new model of 'managed' or 'welfare capitalism' in the UK, one marked by a new balance in the capital/labour relationship and much greater equality. It was a shift largely engineered by the state, but one accepted, at least initially, by big business. In the favourable economic climate of the time, capital ceded ground to the workforce, significant chunks of the economy were taken into public hands, and the share of national output received in wages grew to a new historic high.

This relative harmony between capital and labour – and its equalising force – was not to last. The state and capital used the economic crisis of the mid-1970s to join forces to engineer a new shift in power from labour to capital, and from wages to profits. The share of output paid in wages fell from an average of some 60% in the 1950s and 1960s to around 53% today.[9]

This shift was secured through the weakening of collective bargaining and the suppression of the labour force's influence, the speeding up of deindustrialisation and a rise in the rate of unemployment. In turn, a newly strengthened capital demanded further concessions from government, in areas from regulation and labour rights to taxation, while using its newly given power to impose its dominance on small business suppliers.

Today, the UK's corporate-dominated economy is marked by the overwhelming strength of capital, the weakness of labour and the subservience of the state and small business, and in consequence, the over-rewarding of the owners of capital. Although many factors have been at work, including largely external factors such as globalisation and technological change, it has been the flexing of capital's strength that has been one of the principal drivers of the inequality surge of the last three decades.

At the heart of these issues is the 'distribution question'. How the spoils of the economy should be divided – between employees (through wages and salaries) and the owners of business (through profits and dividends) – is one of the oldest questions in political economy. As one of the founding fathers of modern economics, David Ricardo, wrote in 1821, 'The principal problem in Political Economy' is to determine how 'the produce of the earth … is divided among … the proprietor of the land, the owner of the stock or capital necessary for its cultivation and the labourers by whose industry it is cultivated'.[10]

After the Second World War, the consensus was that developed nations should aim to achieve a higher degree of equality. From the late 1970s, this was displaced by a new orthodoxy, one eventually accepted across the broad political spectrum – from Thatcher to Blair – that egalitarianism had gone too far. Higher inequality, it was claimed is the price we have to pay for a more vibrant economy and faster growth. It is better to have a bigger cake shared less equally, the argument runs, than a smaller one divided more equally. So entrenched was this idea that debate on the distribution question largely disappeared. 'Of the tendencies that are harmful to sound economics', the pro-market theorist and Nobel Laureate, Robert Lucas, pronounced in 2003, 'the most poisonous is to focus on questions of distribution'. Until the 2008 crash, the fundamental question of how the pie should be shared had been largely written out of the political and economic script.

According to pro-market theorists, the boost to corporate pay and the shift from wages to profits – creating a golden age for capital and its owners – should have improved national and global economic health. Yet the evidence says otherwise. The division of the national wealth is a critical factor in ensuring social cohesion. In the post-war years, the more even balance of power, backed by an interventionist state, brought declining rates of both inequality and poverty. Then, the strengthening of capital from the 1980s helped to drive the growing economic divide and rising level of poverty of the last 30 years.

Crucially, the balance between the workforce, capital and government is also a key factor in ensuring economic stability. The greater balance secured in the immediate post-war period contributed to historically high levels of growth, investment and productivity. In contrast, the rise of corporate capitalism has been associated not just with rising inequality, but weakened economic performance and greater turbulence alongside it.

On the one hand, if the share of profits sinks too low, business investment and productivity growth can be stifled. On the other hand, excessively high profit levels can bring a quite different set of distortions. These include the sucking of purchasing power out of the economy, out-of-control incomes at the top, excessive financial surpluses and the over-concentration of economic power. These simply create imbalances that upset the processes of economic equilibrium necessary to prevent instability.[11]

The evidence is that the blind post-1980 experiment in unequal capitalism has failed to bring the promised pay-off of a bigger cake and greater dynamism. The chronic deficit of demand caused by sustained wage compression – and other factors – has helped to make the economy dependent on artificial, but unsustainable stimulants, from escalating rates of personal borrowing to the mass printing of money and state-induced inflation in asset values. This has merely bred fragility and heightened economic risk. The rising profit share since the early 1980s has been associated not with rising private investment and growing productivity, but with an erosion of both. Capital has used its growing muscle not to boost the productive base of the economy but to enrich its owners, leaving economies weaker, squeezing opportunities and raising demands on the social obligations of the state.[12]

There is now a considerable body of research that suggests that inequality was a significant contributory factor in the 2008 crash, that it helped to deepen the recession that followed and to delay recovery, and that it makes economies much more prone to crisis. Highly influential studies by the International Monetary Fund (IMF) have found not only that inequality slows the rate of growth, but that redistribution of wealth does little to harm it: 'Lower net inequality is robustly correlated with faster and more durable growth ... redistribution appears generally benign in terms of its impact on growth; only in extreme cases is there some evidence that it may have direct negative effects on growth.'[13]

The OECD has come to a similar conclusion. It finds that in the two decades up to 2008: 'In Italy, the United Kingdom and the United States, the cumulative growth rate would have been six to nine percentage points higher had income disparities not widened ... On the other hand, greater equality helped increase GDP per capita in Spain, France and Ireland prior to the crisis.'[14]

Above a certain limit, one breached over the last two decades, income polarisation, driven by a steady rise in the return to capital at the expense of the workforce leads to what Guy Ryder, Director-General of the International Labour Organization (ILO), has called a 'dangerous gap between profits and people'.[15]

The growing imbalance between labour, capital and state has brought two key sources of disequilibrium: social and economic. A substantial correction in this relationship is now a necessary condition not just for tackling growing social recession but for achieving sustained economic progress as well.

There have been two key political opportunities to correct this critical imbalance in recent times. The first came with Labour's 1997 election victory. Enjoying a sweeping majority, the first Blair government was in a powerful position to take the public along a path of fundamental reform. It was not to be. New Labour had bought into the model of corporate capitalism. Labour did make some significant reforms, notably through the introduction of the national minimum wage. It also strengthened some employee rights, including the right to paid holidays and better paternity and maternity leave.

Labour also prioritised the tackling of poverty, especially among the workforce, a level that had doubled since the 1970s. But they did so by boosting the generosity of working benefits, rather than through improving the wage share, boosting the workforce's bargaining power or tackling the growing problem of rising housing costs. By allowing inequality to go on rising, the government set out to reduce poverty with one hand tied firmly behind its back. A more generous tax credit system succeeded in raising the net incomes of the growing proportion of the workforce on low wages, but at considerable extra cost in public spending. Almost a quarter of the overall social security bill of just over £200 billion now consists of a state subsidy from taxpayers to employers and to landlords.

The failure to tackle the critical power imbalance between the workforce and employers has come at considerable political cost. It has put additional strain on the state, leading to a new level of public 'over-reach' and pressure on public finances. This is reflected not just in the heavy reliance on working benefits, but also in the growing public antipathy to claimants, benefits and to other aspects of the welfare system. Wage and housing subsidies have, arguably, exceeded their political limits. But there is another side-effect at work. An overburdened state has failed to fulfil another of its critical tasks, that of ensuring an adequate flow of physical and social capital.

The second opportunity for a correction came in the aftermath of the 2008 crash. Many commentators predicted that the severity of the crisis and the prolonged nature of the slump would lead to profound reform, triggered by a similar change in direction that took place in the aftermath of the earlier crises in the 1930s and the 1970s. Here was an opportunity for a major restructuring, aimed at checking the power of financialised capital, building in new checks and balances in the economic system and reinforcing the 'public' side of the still-mixed private–public economy.

Yet that opportunity was also missed. The post-2010 governments have taken us further away from the kind of correction required. Instead of moving to correct the imbalance between the workforce and capital in order to ease the pressure on the protective role of the state, the pendulum has swung yet further in favour of big business. While the banking system has been bailed out, it is the workforce, not the corporate power elite, that has taken most of the battering from 2008 and the subsequent crisis. While executive pay at the top has continued to rise over the last eight years, average wages in the UK were still lower in 2014 than in 2007. This is a much poorer record than nearly all the other member nations of the OECD.[16]

The two post-2010 governments have moved to tackle the over-reach of the state not by imposing greater responsibilities on capital, but by weakening the obligations of the state itself. Key aspects of state social protection for the workforce have been weakened – with a significant scaling back of the more generous safety net introduced by Labour from 1997, and the introduction of a much more punitive benefit system and much tougher conditionality.

Although the government is to introduce a new levy on big business to pay for a boost to apprenticeships, the obligations on capital and the richest sections of society have been further weakened since 2010 by ongoing cuts in corporation tax, cuts in inheritance tax and a range of new measures announced in the 2015 post-election budget to further dilute what is left of trade union power. While the government has announced an increase in the national minimum wage (which the Chancellor cleverly misrepresented as a 'National Living Wage'), the £4 billion addition to the national wage bill will be much more than offset by working-age benefit cuts set to total some £12 billion.

Despite a mounting critique, the model of corporate capitalism remains entrenched. The government is accelerating the pace of privatisation and the outsourcing of public services. Shareholder value – aimed at boosting short-term share values and little more than a supercharged scheme for enriching corporate executives – remains the almost universal corporate goal. In spite of a plethora of high-level inquiries into corporate governance, the executive gravy train continues to roll. Much of the City operates as little more than a cash cow for a small group of executives and financiers. Capital in the UK continues to use its muscle to reward itself and its clients, too often at the cost of taxpayers, employees, small companies and consumers.

That there has been so little policy and so little political reaction to the all too evident and increasingly widely acknowledged flaws in the current economic model, is testament to the power and overdominance of capital.

TWO

Too big to fail: the dominance of private capital

One of the most significant outcomes of these broader trends is the heavily skewed pattern of capital ownership in the UK. The economy is dominated by a single model of enterprise – the large private company. In contrast, the UK has, compared with most other OECD nations, a relatively low level of public, employee and social ownership.[1] The role of public ownership in the UK has been largely reduced to that of an ambulance service, as illustrated by the state rescue of Britain's troubled banks, ones that had presided over years of gross market abuse under private ownership.

Co-operatives account for only 2% of the economy in the UK, compared with 10% in Italy, 19% in Finland, 8% in Germany and around 12% in Switzerland.[2] Only around 100 firms in Britain have full or part employee ownership. They include the logistics company, Unipart, and John Lewis, a partnership which is effectively owned by the company's 76,000 staff and where profits are returned to staff in bonuses. This modest scale is despite the higher rate of sales growth and job creation enjoyed by employee-owned businesses during the recession compared with companies in conventional ownership.[3]

Of course, the large quoted company has a critical role to play in the economy, and has long been a key engine of prosperity. Competition among private firms helps to create wealth and jobs, and capitalism has, along with technological progress and state support, played a central role in raising living standards across the world over most of the last hundred years and longer. Even economies which have had higher levels of public ownership have been moving towards larger private sectors in recent years.[4]

But while competitive markets should continue to play a central role in the economy, healthy competition barely exists in many markets. The private productive base of the economy is highly concentrated. Britain's 100 largest public companies – the FTSE 100 – are collectively worth some four fifths of all the companies in the UK registered on the London Stock Exchange. Further, private equity, in which former quoted companies have been bought up by consortia of wealthy private individuals and deal-making institutions, has become big business, accounting for a fifth of UK employment.

Many key sectors are dominated by a handful of companies. Industries where the top four firms control more than 40% of output (one of the official definitions of an oligopoly) include supermarkets, energy supply, food production, accountancy, banking, soft drinks, pharmaceuticals, electrical retail, and home DIY.[5] The top four supermarkets – Tesco, Asda, Sainsbury's and Morrisons – account for 61% of grocery sales. Four companies – O2, Vodafone, Orange, T-Mobile – almost monopolise mobile phone networks. Despite their indifferent record, four giant accountancy firms – Deloitte, Ernst & Young, KPMG and PricewaterhouseCoopers – retain a stranglehold over the critical role of company auditing in the UK and across the globe.

Amazon has built a giant global company by buying out much of the competition – AbeBooks, LoveFilm, The Book Depository, BookFinder and many more. Amazon's near US$90 billion annual global turnover is greater than the GDP of countries such as Cuba, Oman and Belarus. As a result of its high sales and low wages, the company has built a massive cash reserve.

This increasing market domination of giant firms is a global phenomenon. The market value of the world's top 100 companies – 'an astronomical US$16.2tn' – was, in early 2015, nearly double the value in 2009 ($8.4 trillion). American firms dominate the list, with 53 companies; China has the second most businesses, with 11; while the UK has eight – the third highest ranking.[6] This is all a far cry from the model of competitive market capitalism promoted by pro-market theorists and taught to undergraduates of economics

Britain's corporate sector is also very narrowly owned. As shown in Table 2.1, individuals in the UK owned merely 12% of the shares traded on the London Stock Exchange in 2014, down from 54% in 1963. Shares are held much more transiently than in the past, increasingly by global asset management companies, investment banks and high-frequency traders.[7] The average length of time that shares are held has fallen from six years in 1950 to less than six months today. In this, the UK is on a par with the United States.[8]

Table 2.1: Who owns quoted shares in UK-domiciled companies? (December 2014)

Charities, churches, etc.	1.2%
Banks	1.4%
Investment trusts	1.8%
Private non-financial companies	2.0%
Public sector	2.9%
Pension funds	3.0%
Insurance companies	5.9%
Other financial institutions	7.1%
Unit trusts	9.0%
Individuals	11.9%
Rest of the world	53.8%

Note: Companies that are domiciled overseas are excluded from this analysis
Source: Office for National Statistics, Ownership of Quoted Shares of UK Domiciled Companies, 2014, Table 1

With share ownership increasingly footloose, short-term and detached from corporate influence, the stock market has become little more than a global casino for a small elite. Less than half of households hold private pension schemes, concentrated among the better off.[9] Popular capitalism is a myth. It is also largely a myth that the shareholder value model is necessary to encourage productive investment.[10] In fact, the model actively discourages investment.

Table 2.1 shows that more than a half of shares of listed companies are now owned by foreign investors, making it difficult to talk about the 'British' corporate sector. Over the last decade, more than £200 billion worth of British companies have been sold to global corporations, while a fifth of quoted companies have disappeared from the London Stock Exchange. As the leading economic commentator Will Hutton has argued, Britain has no indigenous quoted company in a range of industries, from cars and chemicals to industrial services and building materials.[11] During 2015, close to a fifth of the UK listed technology sector, including cutting-edge firms like Telecity and Pace, was taken over by overseas (mostly US) companies.

Bypassing the poor

Today's model of corporate capitalism has been forged by a great range of factors. They include:

- decades of rolling privatisation – a process that has gone further in the UK than most other developed countries;
- an antipathy to public ownership and the principle of collectivism;
- a growing boardroom preference to secure growth through corporate mergers and acquisitions;
- a steady reduction in the degree of state regulation of business, notably in controls over the functioning of the labour market and parts of finance;
- a gradual reduction in the level of taxation paid by the corporate sector;

- a weakening of some of the traditional social roles played by corporations, especially in the provision of pensions, apprenticeships and in training.

This process has been compounded too by what the leading political scientist David Marquand has called 'the attrition of the public realm', the erosion of the set of values that serves the public rather than private interest.[12] Big corporations meet a narrow range of interests, and less and less the common good. Increasingly, the provision of key public services as diverse as healthcare, university education and parts of the probation service are being handed over to market forces. With the share of public spending in the economy set to fall to 35% by 2020, local public services and assets from parks to libraries are being slowly starved of funding.

The same forces that have underpinned today's model of corporate capitalism have simultaneously driven the rise in inequality. Of all forms of wealth – from housing to financial assets – it is the distribution of financial wealth (liquid savings and shares) that is most unequal, with a quarter of households left with negative net financial wealth because of accumulated debts.[13]

The gains from growth over the last 30 years have increasingly bypassed the poorest, favouring the top 1% and to a lesser extent the top fifth. This has greatly changed the social and economic structure of society. Since the late 1970s, the share of national income (after tax) taken by the top 1% has increased from 4.7% to 14% and of the top fifth from 35% to 42%. In contrast, the share going to the poorest fifth has fallen from 10% to 8%.[14]

These dramatic shifts in top and bottom shares are intricately linked. Many of the mechanisms that have enriched those at the top have simultaneously contributed to the growing fragility of the labour market, the weakening of opportunities for the most disadvantaged and the spread of impoverishment over the last 30 years.[15]

One of the defining characteristics of the Anglo-Saxon corporate state is the accumulation of economic muscle by a small group of corporate executives and financiers at the expense of ordinary citizens.

Big corporations are increasingly unaccountable to wider society. They are managed largely in the interests of a small, dominant business class, irrespective of the impact on wider society and the economy. Over time, even institutional investors have handed power to corporate executives. Most owners of shares hold them through intermediaries, a fund manager or a passive tracker, and have little direct communication with the firms in which they are investing. A key consequence of this more dispersed and disinterested ownership structure is that it is now harder to exert influence over management. According to Andrew Haldane, the Chief Economist at the Bank of England, this has raised 'the risk of sub-optimal decision-making and of excessive risk-taking.'[16] When pressure is exerted by major shareholders, it is usually to encourage higher dividend payments, rather than boost long-term performance and productivity by raising investment.

This process of power concentration has had a number of negative economic and social effects and is now one of the most pressing issues of progressive political economy.

The diminution of 'counterveiling power'

First, it has contributed to the diminution of what the distinguished US economist JK Galbraith called 'counterveiling power'. The dispersal of power is a vital ingredient of a properly functioning society. Other players, from the workforce to consumers and small businesses, which ought to have a say in the way society is run are unable to influence decisions that can have a dramatic effect on their lives and businesses.

Although small businesses employ more than 15 million people in the UK, they are too often unable to compete on equal terms with large firms. All of the large supermarkets have been involved in exploiting their small suppliers. According to the Federation of Small Businesses, as many as one in five of its members have been the subject of bullying by large corporate customers.[17] Then there's tax. Since the millennium, the effective tax rate paid by multinational corporations has, through the use of complex, hidden and often unchallenged practices, been falling, while the corporate tax bills facing small companies has been rising.[18]

This erosion of historic checks and balances has been particularly strong in the workplace. Driven by a raft of legislation in the 1980s, the level of unionisation in the UK has more than halved over the last 30 years, with an even sharper fall in the private sector. Only one in seven private sector employees is unionised, a much lower figure than the average among rich nations.

Consumers too, have been left with largely token power. The big energy suppliers – able to operate like a loose cartel – regularly top consumer surveys for opaque pricing and for poor experience.[19] Despite the well-documented health risks, and a gathering public concern, the food industry continues to fill too many products with excessive quantities of sugar. British broadband customers pay nearly 50% more than standard prices on the continent.[20] Despite years of high-profile mis-selling scandals, profiteering by Britain's financial services industry in the promotion of savings products continues to be rife. As George Akerlof and Robert Shiller, both Nobel laureates in economics, argue in their book *Phishing for Phools*, 'manipulation and deception' is endemic to corporate practice. Here, they use 'phishing' to mean 'getting people to do things that are in the interest of the phisherman, but not in the interest of the target', that is the customer.[21]

The upward extraction of existing wealth

Second, the power grip enjoyed by corporate capitalism has greatly distorted the pattern of corporate incentives, allowing a growing proportion of economic activity to become associated less with vital 'wealth creation' through the creation of new products, companies and jobs than the upward extraction of existing wealth.

Take executive pay. In spite of a handful of rebellions by shareholders, executive pay carried on rising sharply through the post-2008 crisis years – years of austerity for the bulk of the workforce. In 1998, Britain's chief executives earned 47 times the average worker. By 2010 that figure was 120 times; today it stands at 183. The latest evidence shows that between 1999 and 2013, the median remuneration of a FTSE-100 chief executive rose annually by an average 13.6%. Over the same period, the average annual rise in the FTSE index was just 1.7%.[22]

The continued enrichment of executives inflames not just liberal opinion. 'You don't have to be a Bolshevik to find this huge disparity offensive', raged a 2015 editorial in the *Daily Mail*. 'For in most cases, it owes nothing to merit ... Even ardent champions of capitalism will be appalled that chief executives have helped themselves to an extra £800,000 each, over four years in which they've imposed minimal increases or pay freezes on their employees.'[23]

We can add to this group of corporate executives an army of financial intermediaries, agents and investment managers – the 'marriage brokers' – who earn vast and always opaque fees from arranging deals and oiling the financial wheels of corporate capitalism. The rewards enjoyed by some of this group of mainly City financiers – many of whom have joined the ranks of the *Sunday Times* Rich List – often greatly outstrip those of corporate executives.

Too many trading activities, big business deals and accountancy practices – from merger and acquisition activity to private equity takeovers – have become little more than a zero-sum game. Such activity often adds no new value, but merely transfers existing value from weaker groups (large parts of the workforce and consumers) to a small, powerful business and financial class determined to seize a larger share of the national and global cake for itself, a process labelled 'rent-seeking' by economists. This means that corporate and financial leaders can make more money through rentier activity and short-term financial manipulation than through patient building for higher long-term returns.

The distinction between wealth creation and wealth diversion has long been recognised. Adam Smith, the founder of modern economics, warned in 1776 that because of their love of quick money, 'the prodigals and projectors' could lead the economy astray.[24] In the 1930s it was Keynes who called for the 'euthanasia of the rentier'. In a modern-day equivalent, the World Bank economist Branko Milanovic, has distinguished between 'good' and 'bad' inequality.[25]

In essence, corporate Britain has used its muscle to redistribute existing corporate wealth upwards at the direct expense of company workforces, consumers, savers and often the taxpayer. Much of this activity has, in the process, played havoc with jobs, pay, housing and life chances for the poorest as well as small businesses.

One of the effects of this extraction has been a long-term decline in the flow of private investment, with significant negative consequences for productivity, growth and in turn the balance of payments. Indeed, the rising UK profit share since the late 1970s has been associated with a decline in private investment.[26] The proportion of profit distributed to shareholders has risen seven-fold over the last 45 years, squeezing out private investment. In 1970, £10 out of each £100 of profits was paid to shareholders through dividends. Today, that figure is between £60 and £70, reducing the cash available for growth-boosting investment, and wages.[27]

In part because of low interest rates, big companies in the UK and the US have been issuing record amounts of debt, not to finance future growth but to buy back their own shares, a form of financial engineering that raises earnings per share to the benefit of company executives. In the US, the top 500 companies have spent 2,848% more buying their own shares than investors have moved into the market. In the UK over the past decade, share buybacks by UK companies, financed by a mix of cash reserves and borrowing, have consistently exceeded share issuance. This reduces the number of outstanding shares and raises the level of earnings per share. The prime purpose is to boost share prices, and thus further boost share-price-linked executive pay. Such share buybacks offer short-term gains for a few at the expense of the long-term productive base. Raising the leverage (debt-to-equity ratio) of stocks increases their riskiness and therefore their potential for volatility, thus adding to wider economic instability.[28]

The treatment of employees

Third, more and more companies treat their employees as little more than expendable factors of production, instead of integral to company success. Companies have scaled back the responsibilities they used to take for employees. Company pension schemes have been weakened, as have levels of training and the provision of apprenticeships. British employers spend respectively 70% and 55% less on vocational training than their French and German counterparts.

In some industries, work conditions and benefits have been returning to those of the distant past. Citizens Advice estimates that 460,000 employees have been defined – 'bogusly'– by unscrupulous employers as self-employed, denying them a range of company benefits and rights from holiday pay to parental leave.[29] Amazon, a highly controversial company, imposes what the *New York Times* has called 'punishing' work conditions on its staff. Close to a million work on zero-hour contracts with no guarantee of the number of hours they can work.

The undermining of the democratic process

Fourth, big money has been able to exercise a tightening grip on the political process, contributing to what the annual Audit of British democracy has described as a 'long-term decline' in the state of representative democracy.[30] Corporations, and their highly influential corporate lobby, have been able to wield disproportionate influence over regulation, competition, tax and wider economic policy. Too often, it is the regulated that have captured the regulators. Big business makes huge corporate and individual donations to political parties. There is an ever-revolving door, with senior government officials, former cabinet ministers and private sector executives moving between government, Whitehall, the City and multinational companies.

Tax policy is perhaps the most potent example of 'political capture'. Top corporate tax officials responsible for tax manipulation sit on Treasury committees that draw up the rules on corporate tax avoidance. The level of corporation tax in the UK has fallen from 28% in 2010 to 20% today – the lowest rate among G7 nations – and it is to be cut again to 18% by 2020. In contrast, the current rate in the US is 40%, in France 33.3%, in Germany 29.65%.[31] As a result, the corporate tax take has been falling as a percentage of all tax revenues, from

9.7% in 2000 to under 7% in 2013. In the US, Germany and Italy, corporation tax receipts increased as a percentage of total revenues over the same period.[32]

A catalogue of business scandals

Further, big business has been beset by a long catalogue of scandals, from the rigging of foreign exchange markets by investment banks and the direct exploitation of savers to the growth of aggressive tax avoidance and fleecing of private tenants by landlords and letting agencies. Such scandals have embroiled a long list of giant British and overseas companies, from BP and Tesco to VW.

Corporations become 'too big to fail'

There is another factor at work. Some corporations are so large, and so integrated into the wider economy, that they risk becoming, like the banks, 'too big to fail'. If such companies went down, and not all are economically secure, they would take many other companies with them and have a much wider impact on jobs and other markets. Examples of such companies might include the big insurance companies, mining and trading giants such as Glencore and telecoms like Vodafone.

As the financial magazine *Money Week* has argued, this brings the risk of:

> more and more moral hazard. What that means is that, just as with the banks, there is no real downside for the executives. They can just keep taking extravagant and dangerous risks, confident that if it all goes terribly wrong, the government will have no choice but to step in and rescue them.[33]

The destabilising force of cash surpluses

Finally, a significant consequence of the growing imbalance in the distribution of the national cake has been the build-up of large corporate and private holdings of cash.

In the UK, cash piles held by FTSE 100 corporates, excluding financial companies, stood at £53.5 billion in 2014, with Britain's biggest businesses holding onto cash instead of investing. Worldwide, corporates and private equity firms had amassed a $7 trillion (£4.3 trillion) cash mountain, almost double the figure in 2005.[34]

The growth of these surpluses is explained by a combination of the erosion of wage levels, cuts in the size of company workforces, the more extensive use of tax avoidance schemes and falling levels of private investment. These great pools of money have acted as a powerful destabilising force in recent times. They fuelled speculative activity in the boom that preceded the 2008 crash and then stood largely idle during the post-2008 slump – 'dead money'[35] as Mark Carney called them – thus intensifying the gyration of the recent business cycle.

'Capitalism's apologists'

There is now a growing agreement among a diverse range of policy makers, commentators and business leaders about the flaws with the existing model. In a series of unconventional interventions for an employee of a central bank, the Bank of England's Andy Haldane has been remarkably outspoken on what he sees as the deep-seated weaknesses with Britain's dominant business model, especially its primary goal of delivering short-term hikes in share values, itself a key factor in the accumulation of top fortunes. In May 2015, Haldane acknowledged capitalism's historic strengths, but also spoke of a 'rising tide of criticism of companies' behaviour, from excessive executive remuneration, to unethical practices, to monopoly or oligopoly powers, to short-termism.'[36]

Such concerns are widely shared. Surveys show that a majority of the public no longer trust public companies, especially big ones.[37] A global survey by the Legatum Institute finds capitalism and business lacking support across the world, though notably in the UK, the US and Germany: 'There is an almost universal belief that the world's biggest businesses have cheated and polluted their way to success – with barely ten per cent of respondents in all seven countries surveyed thinking big businesses are "clean"' the Institute concluded.[38]

Such disillusion is reflected in part in the steady growth since the 1960s of a popular desire for new, more individualistic ways of working, free of the hierarchies and constraints imposed by a dominant corporate culture, and with a new emphasis on the 'small'. As one critic has noted, 'Our societies, cultures, politics and economies cluster less and less around a handful of big institutional poles based on hierarchy and established authority and more and more around a multiplicity of small, often informal networks based on self-determination and self-expression.'[39] This desire may be more widely embraced, but it is also difficult to realise in a world so heavily dominated by the control exercised by today's elites and institutions.

Leading investment managers are also sounding the alarm about the malign impact of big business short-termism on the economic base. In early 2015, Larry Fink, Chief Executive Officer of Blackrock – the world's largest asset manager – wrote to the chairmen and CEOs of the top 500 US companies: '[M]ore and more corporate leaders have responded with actions that can deliver immediate returns to shareholders, such as buybacks or dividend increases, while underinvesting in innovation, skilled workforces or essential capital expenditures necessary to sustain long-term growth.'[40]

'Capitalism's biggest enemies aren't the Corbyns, Sanders or Pikettys', wrote former *Conservative Home* editor Tim Montgomerie in the pro-Conservative *Spectator* magazine. 'They are the apologists within capitalism and within capitalist-friendly parties who are complacent and do nothing to combat cronyism, corporate greed and inequality.'[41]

London has hosted two conferences on how to create a more 'inclusive model of capitalism' that 'extends its benefits to all of the system's stakeholders'. These conferences have been attended by a range of senior global political and business leaders and delegates as diverse as former US President Bill Clinton, Mark Carney (the Governor of the Bank of England), the Prince of Wales, and a wide range of corporate chief executives.[42]

Speaking as the first of these conferences in May 2014, Mark Carney nailed his colours firmly to the mast: 'Capitalism loses its sense of moderation when the belief in the power of the market enters the realm of faith … Just as any revolution eats it children, unchecked market fundamentalism can devour the social capital essential for the long-term dynamism of capitalism itself.'[43]

A new and remarkable consensus is now emerging that the present model of political economy is no longer up to the job. It is not just driving unacceptable levels of inequality and poverty, it is also weakening the economic base. It's time should be up.

Yet despite the mounting critique, measures designed to tackle the overdominance of private capital are not even close to the political agenda. As the World Bank's Branco Milanovic has argued: 'If one of the drivers of inequality are capital incomes (and "allied" incomes like those of top management), this is because they are heavily concentrated. "Deconcentration" of capital incomes, that is much wider ownership, particularly of equities, is then a solution. But it is seldom mentioned.'[44]

This is not because of a lack of workable alternatives. The policy measures that could steer us to a more inclusive model that benefits all are clear. Many of them would not just ensure a fairer distribution, but would boost wealth creation as well.

An attempt to create a new, fairer model of capitalism needs to start by embracing the centrality of the 'distribution question'. This means ensuring that GDP growth is more evenly shared through, for example, measures which raise the wage floor and lower the ceiling, while boosting the overall share of the economy paid in wages. This could be achieved through a mix of statutory increases in the minimum wage, measures to encourage more firms to adopt the living wage, a boost to investment in education and training, promoting the bargaining power of workforces (for example, through enabling an employee representative on the board) and strengthening the powers of the Low Pay Commission.

The fall in trade union membership, especially in the private sector, means that the great majority of private employees have no collective say in their conditions of employment. Far from being a strength, this decline is a sign of democratic weakness. Because of the 'wage premium' associated with collective bargaining, the erosion of labour force power has been a significant factor in the falling wage share since 1980.[45]

A new democratic settlement would aim to spread power as a counter to big business – to consumers, the workforce and small business. Central too is the need to remodel the financial services industry, with new measures to check rent-seeking activity and steer more resources into wealth creation through greater financial support for investment.

Inclusive capitalism would also require major reforms of taxation. The returns to capital need to be more adequately taxed. This would require a shift in the pattern of taxation with, for example, a more potent tax on capital gains and on the transfer of wealth, possibly through the introduction of a lifetime's capital receipts tax.[46] It would also require a much tougher war on corporate and private tax avoidance, buttressed by a greater emphasis on international cooperation. While taxing capital was highly effective in the post-war years in helping to reduce wealth inequality and building a more progressive tax system, tax rates on wealth, inheritance, corporate profits and personal assets have been falling in the UK and across the globe, resulting in the relative under-taxation of capital and wealth compared with income.

This is the route proposed by Thomas Piketty in his book *Capital in the Twenty-First Century*. Piketty advocates a comprehensive international agreement to establish a progressive tax on individual wealth. Nevertheless, he also acknowledges that the idea is somewhat 'utopian'. Such an idea is not on the political agenda in the great majority of nations or global institutions such as the European Union.[47]

Finally, measures are needed which encourage a greater role for socialisation of the economy, with a higher degree of capital collectively owned. A move in this direction is also advocated by Piketty. As he puts it, '... one of the most important issues in coming years will be the development of new forms of property and democratic control of capital'.[48] This could be achieved in part by encouraging other business models through partnerships, social and mutual enterprises and cooperatives.

There is also a strong case for greater public ownership. The privatisation process has had very mixed success. In the energy market, for example, 'competition' has simply brought confusion with big questions over pricing, profitability and the quality of service.[49] Many countries – from Germany to Singapore – have higher levels of state ownership of key industries. In Singapore, despite its reputation as a free-market haven, a fifth of business activity is in public ownership, as is 85% of housing. The level of privatisation has proceeded more slowly in most countries than in the UK, while many countries that have privatised key utilities have started to reverse the process.

Paradoxically, substantial chunks of the UK's privatised utilities – from transport services and energy supply – are now owned by overseas state industries. Britain's power supply infrastructure is now in the hands of the French government-owned EDF. As one critic has written, 'France in effect renationalised the (power) industry its neighbour had so painstakingly privatised. Renationalised it, that is, for France.'[50]

Creating a more inclusive model of capitalism, one that delivers benefits for all and not the few and simultaneously builds a more productive economic base, would require movement on all these fronts. Yet few of these measures are even close to the mainstream political agenda. A shift in the balance of power away from capital does not look, at the moment, remotely likely. The rate of capital taxation is likely to continue to fall. There is at best a token acknowledgment of the importance of the 'distribution question'.

There is, however, another route that could make an important contribution to building a more inclusive economy while reducing inequality and which could command popular support. This is through the creation of collectively owned social wealth funds. It is their potential to become a powerful weapon for tackling the twin problems of inequality and economic sclerosis that is examined in the remaining chapters.

Such funds would help to limit the extent of private ownership, while ensuring that the returns to ownership would be more widely shared. Some models could capture some of the financial gains from capital growth and use the proceeds for wider benefit..

Such funds should be seen as complementary to these other policy approaches, not as a substitute. They could, for example, sit side by side with the extension of alternative, mutual and cooperative forms of business ownership, and with measures that reverse wage compression. They are already used across a range of nations, and have a crucial role to play in modern economies, independently of the effectiveness of these wider strategies.

So would it be possible to build one or more such collectively owned funds in the UK, and if so, how should they be financed? As well as funding social investment and anti-inequality programmes, could a targeted fund also help to finance a regular payment to citizens, maybe an annual dividend, or even a regular citizen's income?

THREE

Fair shares: social wealth funds and the sharing of national wealth

Social wealth funds are collectively held financial funds, fully owned by the public and used for the benefit of society as a whole. If properly structured, such funds could contribute to a wider spread of the ownership of capital and its benefits. Funds could also be created which accumulate a share of private capital growth over time. Such funds would set out to mobilise pools of existing resources and capital, from the potential returns from publicly owned assets to parts of existing tax revenue, to meet the goals of a sharing economy and fill some of the growing gaps in existing public provision.

The building of such funds would contribute to a much needed correction in the imbalance between labour, capital and the state. By cutting back the growth of private wealth and by being used to promote wider opportunities, such funds could also tackle the income and opportunity gap from both ends.

The funds could play a key role in tackling the distribution question and achieving a more equal division of the economic cake. They are a way of ensuring that income from economic activity is shared more evenly before the application of redistributive taxation and the payment of social benefits, thus taking some of the pressure off the redistributive role of the state. The impact and scope of such funds depends on how they are financed and used. They could be established at a national and regional level and help to pay for infrastructure investment and urban regeneration. They could also help to fund measures that aided upward social mobility through, for example, tackling youth and long-term unemployment, such as by the use of guaranteed employment programmes, or to fund more scholarships and bursaries for disadvantaged young people.

Such funds would be technically owned by the state, but the key to their success is that they should be fully transparent, with details of their size, source of funding, goals and use made accessible to the public. If they were run merely as a remote addition to Britain's already often unresponsive centralised state, they would not gain the public support necessary to make them work. Once established, the funds should mostly be managed independently of the state through, for example, a mix of representatives from local government, charitable organisations, trade unions and the regions, as well as representatives of government and business, and possibly the general public. The National Lottery Fund, for example, providing finance for a range of 'good causes' is run by a non-departmental public body, governed by a nine-strong board. In this sense, social wealth funds would play a very different role from traditional models of public ownership.

Clearly, such funds could not offer solutions to all the growing range of problems associated with corporate capitalism. However, as well as standing alone, they could play a central role in a wider package of reforms aimed at creating an alternative, progressive economic and social strategy.

They would provide an opportunity to raise the proportion of the economy held in collective ownership, with their returns shared across the population. They could help to reverse the long-term trend towards the privatisation of formerly commonly held resources and could open up a greater share of economic activity to public awareness. Such funds could also help to align the interests of society and business more closely and could be managed in ways that contributed to the wider dispersal of power. If their assets included individual stakes in companies, for example, their role could be extended to influencing boardroom decision making in areas such as employee working conditions.

Public social funds should, in most cases, be allowed to grow over time with only a proportion of the fund's value used each year. In this way, part of the funds would be reinvested in a variety of asset classes from bonds and equities to redevelopment schemes. This would be similar to the way private pension funds build up reserves to cover their future liabilities and is the key to the longevity of many charitable foundations. In this way, their benefits would be spread across generations. The potential is well illustrated by the scale of assets (currently worth over £40 billion) accumulated by the diverse range of charitable foundations – from the Wellcome Trust to the Leverhulme Trust – in the UK.[1] Such foundations, mostly financed by private legacies, have grown over time and today fund a great diversity of causes.

If the funds were managed to grow in this way, they would, once established, boost the value of publicly owned assets, thus playing a crucial supporting role in wider macroeconomic management. By adding over time to the pool of public assets, they would help to improve the overall balance sheet of the public finances, a side of the economy almost completely, and seemingly deliberately, ignored in today's one-sided debate about the scale of the national debt. Such debt would be much less of an issue if it was supported by national, publicly owned wealth in the form of infrastructure, public financial and real assets. In recent years, the debate has been almost wholly confined to one side of the equation – reducing the national debt.

As the leading economist Sir Tony Atkinson has shown in his book *Inequality*, the net worth of the public sector – total public assets minus the national debt – has shifted sharply since the mid-1950s. In 1957, this figure was negative – the national debt exceeded the value of state assets by the equivalent of a third of national income. This balance then improved significantly, so that by the late 1970s, the public net worth was positive at around three-quarters of national income. Since then the picture has deteriorated, largely because of the sell-off (at a significant discount) of large chunks of public housing and of publicly owned corporations, from British Telecom to the Royal Mail. In 2007, the net worth was still positive at around a quarter. By 2013, because of the loss of these public assets and the rise since 2008 in the national debt, that figure was negative, at around minus a quarter.[2]

Held in common

One of the key advantages of social wealth funds is that they embrace the central principle that at least part of the gains from economic activity should be shared more equally across society. Some of these gains arise purely from individual effort, skill and risk taking. But a significant proportion stem from communal activity or decision making. This holds, for example, when such gains are the product of the development of natural resources, such as land or oil and gas reserves which are, or should be, commonly owned.

As early as 1795, the British-born radical philosopher and champion of democracy and human rights, Thomas Paine, argued that land and other natural resources are in effect common property, owned by all of a country's citizens. At least part of the benefit should therefore be shared among those citizens. 'Every individual in the world is born therein with legitimate claims on a certain kind of property, or its equivalent,' Paine wrote in *Agrarian Justice*, a short pamphlet about property rights. 'The earth,' he continued, 'in its natural, cultivated state was, and ever would have continued to be the common property of the human race. In that state every man … would have been a joint life proprietor …'[3]

Take land. Because it is part of the natural wealth of society, inherited by each generation, the financial gains from its use should be shared within and across generations. Those who use or occupy it in this way, Paine argued, should pay ground rent to the whole community. Since then, economists have generalised from the profits that landowners reap from the occupation of land into the concept of 'economic rent': if someone uses natural resources that belong to all of us in order to make money for themselves, then some of the gains will take the form of 'economic rent'.

The concept of sharing gains should apply in a range of other circumstances. There are, for example, multiple pools of such common wealth, not just land and natural resources such as oil and gas, water and the atmosphere but, as some have suggested, the electromagnetic spectrum, the copyright system, limited space for airport landing slots and parts of the financial system.[4] Other occasions when it would be legitimate for such gains to be fully or partly shared include when they arise from the exploitation of disproportionate economic power, when they are co-created by external social decisions and actions rather than by the exclusive efforts or skill of individual people or organisations, or when they are simply unearned.

The role of accident and chance in the process of enrichment was recognised by Friedrich Hayek, the highly influential Austrian free-market economist and Nobel Laureate.[5] In any economy, parts – sometimes large parts – of the gains from commercial and financial activity are essentially unearned, the product of one or more of luck, manipulation and wider economic and political decisions.

- Some of these gains – those that accrue to landowners, and inheriting heirs, for example – are the result of the accident of birth.
- Some arise from the exercise of monopoly or near-monopoly power and the manipulation of industrial muscle.
- Others derive from community planning decisions.
- Much private activity is helped, directly or indirectly, through publicly financed support, not just through 'corporate welfare', including direct subsidies, but also through tax-funded education and health systems and the transport and legal infrastructure.

The ownership of land confers huge financial advantages, often unearned. Because land ownership remains more heavily concentrated than almost any other economic asset, the gains from rocketing land prices have ended up in the pockets of a very small and privileged group. While large chunks of land in the UK have been sold off over the last century, in recent years to a new plutocracy including a mix of Russian oligarchs and oil sheikhs, land ownership is still heavily concentrated.[6]

Land development is a highly lucrative business. Agricultural land sold for housing or other development can bring huge rewards for its owners, mainly because of the artificial scarcity created by a combination of tough planning laws, unequal ownership and generous tax exemptions and farm subsidies.

Soaring commercial rents and land values in property hotspots are mostly the direct result of wider planning and transport policies, with the benefits confined to a few. It is these policy decisions which give land its added value – from the granting of development to mineral rights and provision of facilities such as schools – yet most of that extra value goes to the individual landowner rather than back to wider society.

In his book *Taken For a Ride*, the property developer Don Riley showed how surrounding land values along the new Jubilee Tube line corridor in London rose by £1.3 billion per station, largely untaxed windfall gains that accrued to local landowners just by virtue of ownership and a public planning decision.[7] Overall, the cost of land in the UK has risen from a quarter to a half of the total building cost of the average home over the last 40 years.

A wide range of business activity generates unearned gains. Airlines and airports generate economic rent for their owners because of lack of capacity. So do industries with disproportionate levels of concentration. Then there is the application of corporate manipulation to boost executive rewards. Examples include the mis-selling of savings products, the financial engineering of corporate accounts and the recent growth of large-scale share buybacks.

Large windfall gains have also accrued from the boost to share values generated by the mass printing of money (quantitative easing – QE) in the UK, the US, Japan and the EU and the artificially low interest rates that followed the 2008 crash. The FTSE 100 index almost doubled in value (from 3,542 to 6,500) in the six years from the day of the launch of QE in March 2009 (though it fell around 5% during 2015). The rise from 2008 was not the product of a surge in corporate performance. Indeed, the real economy continued to struggle over most of this period.

In the US, the Standard & Poor's 500 rose by around 200% during their three rounds of QE, greatly outstripping the underlying rate of economic growth, leading to what most commentators regard as greatly overinflated values for some companies, especially tech companies.[8] This gain, and the gain in other asset values, including property values in major cities across the world, is primarily the result of artificial stimulants, especially market-friendly monetary policies, yet the gains have mainly benefited the existing, already wealthy, asset-owning class.

Policy measures

Over time, a number of policy measures have been used in the UK and other countries to capture and pool some of these gains for wider community use. These include public ownership, regulation, taxation and direct public provision. The principle of achieving greater fairness in the distribution of gain was at the heart of much post-war state intervention, from the nationalisation of industries and utilities with a strong element of public interest to the provision of public housing aimed at dealing with the inability of markets to deliver a sufficient number of affordable homes. Taxation and direct corporate payments have also been widely used as a way of ensuring that the gains from common resources can be tapped for community benefit.

One of the most recent examples was the charge imposed by the Treasury in 2000 for the use of the radio spectrum for the third generation of mobile phones. The auctioning of these rights and the granting of 20-year licences raised a pretty hefty £22.5 billion.

While the principle of 'common distribution' – that unearned gains should be more evenly shared – has been long accepted, it has been very weakly applied in practice. Attempts to achieve the socialisation of gains have mostly been very limited, including in the case of land. Governments have long grappled with the land question and how to handle the increases in wealth that derive not from personal investment or effort but from wider community decisions and activity. The first political attempt to introduce a tax on developmental gain in the UK came with David Lloyd George's 1909 tax on windfall gains. But the tax was mild and was repealed in 1920.[9] A 1942 proposal for some kind of land nationalisation was watered down by the post-war Labour government. The 1966 Labour government attempted to introduce a development land tax, but it was dismantled by the incoming Conservatives in 1970. In 2005, Labour considered introducing a 'planning gain supplement' – a tax on the gains from property development to help fund infrastructure projects needed to build new houses. The idea, suggested by economist Kate Barker in her 2004 report into housing supply, was bitterly fought by the construction industry and finally dropped.[10]

One way of capturing development gains would be through the creation of public or community-owned land banks. Such banks operate in several countries, such as South Korea, Singapore, Taiwan and Hong Kong, as national agencies playing a major role in national growth strategies, urban development and managing house price inflation. Such banks buy land cheaply on the open market before planning permission and then sell it for future property development once permission has been granted. In Korea, for example, this approach has been responsible for around half of residential development and almost all industrial land development in the country, and has been a key factor in ensuring adequate housing supply. Crucially, this approach ensures that any planning gain – the rise in price from the granting of planning permission – is captured by the publicly owned land bank fund and not by developers.[11] A number of European nations, including Sweden and France, operate advance land acquisition policies to secure public benefit from urban development.

An alternative approach would be the introduction of a land value tax (LVT) – with property owners and landowners paying an annual levy based on the market value of their land. An LVT would replace the regressive hotchpotch of current property taxation: stamp duty, council tax and even business rates. It would be another direct way of collecting the 'economic rent' from land ownership.

The idea of LVT is centuries old. It has been advocated by Adam Smith, by the American radical economist Henry George in 1879 and even by Winston Churchill. 'Unearned increments in land are not the only form of unearned or undeserved profit, but they are the principal form of unearned increment,' Churchill declared in a speech outside the House of Commons in 1909, 'and they are derived from processes which are … positively detrimental to the general public.'[12] The pro-market economist and Nobel Laureate Milton Friedman once called it the 'least bad tax', and it has more recently been backed by the 2011 Mirrlees Review of the UK tax system.[13]

Progressive property variants of LVT are applied in a number of countries. Danish citizens pay 1% of the value of their property to the state for the first DKK3.04 million (£343,000) of its value and 3% for anything over that. In Singapore, those living in expensive properties pay 15% a year. Most US states have a property tax of one kind or another (the highest close to 2%) and Pennsylvania even has something close to a real LVT, in that many of its cities collect tax at a higher rate on land than they do on the buildings themselves.

The principle that windfall development gain should be more evenly shared between landowners and the community is very widely accepted. Indeed, in the UK there is now a coalition calling for government 'to put in place a mechanism whereby a proportion of this increase in land value is used to fund public goods', backed not just by Shelter, the Royal Town Planning Institute and the National Housing Federation but also by the right-of-centre thank tanks, the Institute of Economic Affairs and ResPublica.[14]

Yet, despite its merits, and heritage of support, an LVT is not close to the political agenda, partly because of the practical issues involved, including the complexities of valuing land and separating it from the value of housing. There is also the power of a home ownership lobby heavily opposed to measures that would manage house prices down.[15] Of course, the political climate may change. Apart from the wider merits of a progressive property tax, the debate is moving in the direction of shifting from taxes on income to taxes on wealth, and that will include property.

Social wealth funds and the sharing of economic gain

With some exceptions, only a small proportion of the unearned gains from the exploitation of common wealth have been widely shared. Indeed, an implicit assumption of today's somewhat dogmatic belief in the virtues of private ownership is that the fruits of capital and land (and home ownership) should be exclusive to the owners, rather than at least some of it shared with wider society.

More and more of the economy is privately owned, with the economic rent from a very wide spread of activity mostly very exclusively distributed. Some of the biggest businesses in the world succeed almost entirely by drawing on such common resources. Governments have increasingly handed over exclusive rights to corporations to develop natural resources, pocketing the profits and paying little to the community in return. Today, more and more is simply extracted by a very nimble corporate sector, rather than shared fairly among citizens. At the same time, the damaging social and environmental costs of this process are largely borne by the public or the biosphere.[16]

In general, the principle of socialisation, despite its wider benefits, has been greatly eroded in recent decades, with a growing emphasis on individual provision and payment. Social house building has fallen to a trickle. Public ownership has been scaled back. A growing proportion of private pension arrangements have dropped the principle of collective risk, replaced by the rise of personal pensions and essentially individualised company pension schemes where the risk associated with future returns is borne by the individual and not shared.

The dominance of corporate capitalism and the culture of individualism have ensured that these issues – who should own what and how the gains from whole swathes of economic activity should be allocated – have been largely dropped from mainstream political and economic debate. Instead, the orthodoxy remains that, in order to improve economic performance and bolster incentives, the economy should be mostly privately owned, with these rewards belonging exclusively or heavily to corporate owners to do with as they wish.

Capital has, as a result, become more lightly taxed and regulated, while the traditional justifications for encouraging such freedom – that it is necessary to promote faster growth, greater efficiency, and to boost private investment – have become increasingly weak.[17]

Social wealth funds offer a potentially powerful way of putting the principles of shared distribution and socialisation into practice. The evidence is that both principles have wide public support. Although they have been less widely applied in recent years, they remain at the heart of key areas of public and social provision from planning (designed to control development for the collective benefit), health and education to the public pension funds run by public organisations.

Such provision recognises that there can be a net social gain when citizens come together to provide collective solutions to social and economic problems, with obligations, risks and benefits shared across society, and certain key activities managed for the common good, not just a minority of citizens.

Common ownership is practised by voluntary associations, charities and non-profit organisations such as housing associations and trusts. Most cooperatives have some element of common ownership, although some part of their capital may be individually owned. The John Lewis partnership is one of Britain's most popular companies.

Social wealth funds would challenge the idea that an ever-higher proportion of economic activity should be built around private ownership, embracing instead the idea that more of a country's wealth should be held in common, with the benefits widely shared. Such funds offer an effective and potentially popular alternative way of capturing and distributing economic and social gains. Social wealth funds should not be seen as a way of displacing other measures for socialising unearned private gains. Instead they could complement traditional measures such as regulation and taxation. Further, taxation of such gains would be an important source of finance for such funds.

Many countries have already gone down this route, setting up sovereign wealth funds financed by some of the gains from productive activity arising from natural resources. These are a direct way of ensuring that natural resources are managed in a way that benefits all.

Many of today's most glaring social and economic problems – the chronic lack of adequate and affordable housing, the poor and variable quality of social care, low public and private investment – are a sign of the inadequacy of relying heavily on market forces. The establishment of targeted social wealth funds could play a key role in boosting public provision in areas as diverse as social housing and infrastructural investment. The potential for such funds and how they might be financed and used are discussed in more detail in Chapter Five.

Such funds have an established history. Variants of them have been created in a number of countries and circumstances. Despite this, and their multiple merits, the UK has yet to join the social wealth fund club.

FOUR

The international experience: what can we learn?

There is nothing especially new nor utopian about social wealth funds.

They were first used in the United States in the mid-19th century to fund specific local public services.[1] The state of Texas, for example, established The Permanent School Fund in 1854, with a $2,000,000 grant by the Texas Legislature, to fund primary and secondary schools. In 1876, this idea was extended to universities, with the Permanent University Fund being endowed with public lands.[2]

Today, the School Fund is valued at close to $38 billion, making it the US's largest educational endowment. It is used to help pay for school district costs, is overseen by the Land Commissioner's office and the State Board of Education, and receives a percentage of the proceeds from the sale of state land and rental of mineral rights for oil and natural gas exploration.

Since this pioneering step, a great variety of schemes have been implemented, though there are substantial differences between them. Some of them are much more suitable as a blueprint than others.

Sovereign wealth funds

The dominant form of state asset pooling is the sovereign wealth fund, in which assets are collected in a single fund and invested to generate returns for the state. Today there are over 70 such funds worldwide, up from around 15 in the mid-1990s. Most have been established since the millennium, with total assets in 2015 approaching US$7 trillion.[3] These funds are made up of a great diversity of assets, from equities, bonds and property to investments in precious metals and infrastructure projects.

In nearly all cases, these funds have been financed by a mix of trade surpluses and profits and dividends from oil wealth, sometimes through public ownership and sometimes from taxation of private companies developing the assets. In the Gulf States, the original aim was to lower the foreign exchange and investment risks associated with huge trade surpluses from mass oil reserves, cash that would otherwise have sat idly in treasury accounts. Others were conceived as stabilisation funds to protect economies from large revenue swings.[4]

Many of the sovereign wealth funds have enjoyed significant growth, while a number have been managed by British asset managers, such as Aberdeen Asset Management. This growth has given some countries huge fiscal power, and has been made possible by the partial reinvestment of these sums over many years. Much of the growth is down to the great surge in the oil price from the mid-1990s, athough the sharp fall in prices during 2015 has dented the value of most of the funds, forcing governments to sell parts of the portfolios. Countries with such funds include China (with four funds with a combined value of US$1.3 trillion), the United Arab Emirates (with funds totaling more than US$700 billion), Saudi Arabia (with US$668.0 billion), Kuwait (Kuwait Investment Authority with US$592.0 billion) and Singapore, Russia, Qatar and Australia. Although there is no US federal fund, several states, many of them conservative run, have established funds. They include Alabama, Nebraska, New Mexico, Texas and Wyoming. The socialised Permanent Wyoming Mineral Trust Fund, for example, has a market value of some $7 billion; accumulated from mineral extraction, the fund has helped to reduce taxes in the state.

There are significant variations in the origins, goals and practice of such funds. What they have in common is that they are state-owned financial vehicles for managing large-scale public funds. The gains from such funds have been used in diverse ways. Some are run directly by members of the ruling families of the Gulf States and have contributed to the huge personal wealth accumulated by their governing elites; others have been used to help with fiscal stabilisation by relieving shortfalls in a state's fiscal position, to support national pension schemes or health services and other public services without needing to increase tax revenue, or to aid long-term economic and social development. The Singapore fund, for example, originally set up to manage the exchange rate risk of running large (non-oil) trade surpluses, is now used to support investment in business development and infrastructure.

In an era of increasingly concentrated capital ownership in much of the developed and developing world, the massive wealth pools held by some of these sovereign wealth funds have the potential to promote a more equitable distribution of capital than markets are able to achieve, while enriching and empowering citizens other than through traditional programmes of redistribution. In reality, few countries are using their funds for this purpose.

These existing funds can be distinguished between those which are simply state sovereign funds with very limited social goals and those which are social wealth funds, aimed specifically at socialising wealth in order to benefit wider society. The majority fall into the first category, operating primarily as the investment arm of the state with limited wider benefit. Many claim to have wider social goals: that, for example, the funds are being used to facilitate a transfer of wealth from one generation to the next to ensure that some of the benefits are preserved for future as well as current generations. But these claims are mostly overstated. Few have been explicitly used as instruments for encouraging improved societal welfare. Despite a voluntary code of conduct (the 2008 Santiago Principles) governing how they should operate,[5] sovereign wealth funds are often extremely secretive and many are highly controversial. Most are run in a very closed and non-transparent way, with minimal or no public involvement.

Many, notably the large Chinese and Middle Eastern funds, have used their substantial chequebooks to invest heavily in the United

States, Africa and Europe, including the UK. These have bought shares in companies (or in some cases whole companies), financed takeover bids, and invested in urban redevelopment and large luxury property developments. Many of the biggest property development schemes in the UK have been financed in this way. Sovereign wealth funds, for example, have invested more in the London property market than they have in Tokyo, Paris and New York combined.[6]

The Qatar fund owns the £3 billion Chelsea Barracks and (with a Canadian partner) the £2.6 billion Canary Wharf sites, adding to a vast London property empire that includes Harrods and the Shard. Both the China Investment Corporation and the Abu Dhabi Investment Authority (ADIA) have taken stakes in Thames Water, while ADIA owns The Lanesborough – the Regency-style Hyde Park Corner hotel favoured by Russian oligarchs, and in 2013 bought 42 regional Marriott hotels from Royal Bank of Scotland, in a deal worth a reported £640 million.

It is significant that successive British governments, desperate to boost infrastructure spending, have deliberately encouraged such investments. In 2012, the former Commercial Secretary to the Treasury, Lord Sassoon, reported a 'huge appetite' for British infrastructure among sovereign funds in the Gulf.[7]

Nevertheless, such investment should come with a big health warning. Amnesty International and Human Rights Watch have long protested against the human rights record in countries such as Abu Dhabi and China. Human Rights Watch has accused one gulf state of using ownership of British assets to 'construct a public relations image of a progressive, dynamic Gulf state, which deflects attention from what is really going on in the country'.[8]

Encouraging large-scale foreign investment may bring short-term fiscal gains, such as a lower reliance on public borrowing. But some forms of investment can have negative side effects, with some big property deals greatly distorting the residential housing market away from balanced development. Moreover, by making the UK vulnerable to the whims of foreign state investors, such investment carries economic and political risks. The decision to allow a Chinese–French consortium to pay for, build and control three nuclear power stations does not involve risk taking by the Chinese, as the project will be heavily subsidised and the returns guaranteed, with the bill falling on UK consumers and taxpayers. Such reliance is a classic example of political short-termism, which risks large and uncertain long-term costs.

There is always going to be uncertainty about the medium- and long-term intentions behind some of these investments. As the think tank the Intergenerational Foundation has warned, sovereign wealth funds are:

> above all, political beasts. Britain's infrastructure is of strategic importance: a public good. Do we want to hitch our roads, broadband, electricity and so forth to the economic stability of the autocratic Wild East? The Arab Spring has shown the speed at which entire systems can be overthrown. Many questions surround the government's confident assertion that the [sovereign wealth funds] can fill the gap.[9]

One of the negative consequences of growing dependency on foreign investment – on the trade deficit – is becoming all too apparent. That deficit now stands at 5% of GDP, the worst performance since records began. The problem has been greatly exacerbated by the growing gap between the money we earn on British-owned businesses abroad and the profits sent to overseas owners of foreign-owned businesses located here – the likes of Jaguar Land Rover, Heathrow and Cadbury. The income generated by our overseas investments *fell* 31% between 2011 and 2014 to £73 billion, while the amount sent to overseas owners of British-based assets *rose* by 31% to £71 billion. The previous surplus on this account fell from £54 billion in 2011 to £2 billion in 2014.

The main explanation for this deterioration lies in the growing value of UK assets held by foreign owners, the result, as Anthony Hilton of the *Evening Standard* has called it, of 'the willingness of the UK to sell anything that moves to a foreign buyer with a big chequebook.'[10] The UK may gain in the short term from the influx of capital and skills, but is now beginning to pay a heavy price for this short-termism: the UK's overseas assets are now worth less than the total now owned by the rest of the world.

Such is the size of some of these funds, and the scale of their combined wealth, that they have become big and powerful economic players on the world stage. Some commentators argue that sovereign wealth is being used to secure economic imperialism, creating, as one critic has put it, a 'shadow market' in the provision of liquidity and investment cash, able, by stealth, to use their pile of capital 'to seize geopolitical power'.[11] What is also clear is that sovereign wealth funds are targeting the economic rents that have, in recent times, largely been the preserve of individual and corporate players. While the British government is bending over backwards to encourage them to do so, other major nations, from Germany and France to the US, seek to protect strategic investment.

Because of the lack of transparency, the narrow basis of control and the questionable uses to which the funds are sometimes put, many of these funds fall well short of meeting the criteria for a model social wealth or a community fund – notably on transparency and public accountability, on the nature of investment, and on how the proceeds are spent and distributed. As one analyst, Angela Cummine, has concluded: 'With some isolated exceptions, citizens are largely quarantined from exerting any direct influence over or enjoying any direct benefit from the management, investment and distribution of "their" sovereign wealth.'[12]

Funds in New Zealand, Norway and France

Only a handful of existing funds come close to being described as 'social wealth funds'. Perhaps the closest, those that meet a range of desirable criteria, are those operating in New Zealand, Norway and Alaska (the latter to be discussed later in this chapter). These funds are more open and transparent, with more clearly declared economic and social goals. Their primary aims are a long way from economic imperialism. None of them offers direct public involvement with the public (through referenda or consultative mechanisms) electing managements, or having a representative voice, or having a say on goals and investment policy. Nevertheless, while they could not be called full or partial community funds (ones with some measure of direct public involvement), they do offer extensive public disclosure. All have the effect of contributing to a more equal distribution of the gains from resource production.

Although the New Zealand fund is still relatively small – worth some US$20 billion – it achieved one of the highest rates of return among sovereign wealth funds between 2010 and 2015. The fund was set up in 2001 by the then Labour government in New Zealand essentially to accumulate resources to help cover future pension liabilities. It is run by a group called the 'Guardians', which enjoys considerable autonomy from government, operates with an emphasis on long-term returns and is now globally recognised for its innovative approach to investment. Over a fifth of the fund is invested in long-term illiquid assets, such as timber and farmland.

One of the nearest to a model fund is found in Norway. The nation in fact runs two funds. Established in the 1980s, their primary aim has been to ensure that the benefits of North Sea oil production would be spread across generations. They are managed by the Norwegian central bank on behalf of the Norwegian people. The Norwegian funds now regularly top international rankings for transparency, but have not always been free of controversy.[13] In the 1990s they received much negative publicity for investing in a Singaporean company involved in the production of anti-personnel mines. In response, the government set up an expert Council of Ethics to develop investment guidelines and monitor its activities. In recent years, the fund has sold its shares in a number of companies that have failed to meet its set ethical standards. Only Norway and New Zealand have established such ethical scrutiny.[14]

The Norwegian fund's income stems from several sources:

• directly from its ownership of several oil fields;
• indirect taxes on oil and gas;

- dividends from a majority stake in Statoil, the country's largest energy company;
- returns on its investments.

While determined to ensure that the fund makes money, its managers place a high premium on achieving legitimacy, by focusing on traditional issues of corporate governance, encouraging shareholder rights and board accountability in companies it invests in. It has also used its shareholder muscle to influence corporate behavior. Among the issues it monitors closely are child labour, water management and climate change, issues that have won it plaudits from humanitarian groups and corporate governance advocates around the world. Because of its openness, and shareholder activism, it enjoys a good deal of public support, legitimacy and global recognition. 'The fund, one of the most transparent, least secretive investment vehicles in the world, operates under stringent disclosure requirements, and has become a shareholder activist, aggressively pushing the businesses it invests in to follow healthy corporate governance practices.'[15]

Norway's approach is in stark contrast to that of the UK, which has also had the benefit of significant oil and gas reserves – 'God's gift to the British economy', as the Labour Prime Minister Jim Callaghan once described such reserves. Instead of using part of the gain for the future by investing some of the tax revenues raised, British governments have chosen to spend the proceeds in tax cuts and current consumption and allowing the exchange rate to rise. The UK and Norway, by an accident of geography, have both been sitting on a large pot of black gold. The UK has spent it; Norway has saved it. While Norway now has big cash reserves as a result, the UK has been a net importer of oil for a decade, and has faced a worsening and critical balance of payments deficit and decline in tax revenues, without a wealth fund to soften the blow. At their 1980s' peak, the UK's North Sea oil and gas revenues were worth around 3% of the economy. To date, the UK has extracted some 42 billion barrels generating around £400 billion (in current real prices) in tax revenue.

There have been several estimates of what a fund could have been worth if this tax revenue had been invested for the long term. PricewaterhouseCoopers has estimated that such a fund would have been worth £450 billion by 2008 (that's bigger than the wealth funds of Kuwait, Qatar and Russia combined).[16] Another estimate suggests it might have been closer to £850 billion by now, the equivalent of some £13,000 per person.[17] The economist Tony Atkinson puts the figure somewhat lower – in the order of £350 billion today.[18] If the UK had gone down this road, creating its own 'rainy-day' fund, the public sector net worth would now be positive instead of negative. There would be considerably less panic about the national debt, and the UK economy would be operating on a more secure footing. Today there is, rightly, much gnashing of teeth about corporate short-termism, yet governments are just as culpable and have fewer excuses.

Together, Norway's funds are estimated to hold a remarkable 1% of global equities and are, jointly, the largest stock owners in Europe. When the first fund was started, politicians envisaged it lasting for maybe 30 years. Now it is set to last decades more. This longevity is largely down to the rule that the fund can only spend the annual gains (up to a maximum of 4% of the funds), continuing to reinvest the rest, thus ensuring that future generations benefit from the oil legacy.

In 2008, France joined this short list with its own structural investment fund. It is currently worth some US$25 billion, at the lower end of the sovereign wealth fund league. The fund was established by President Nicolas Sarkozy as a direct response to the burgeoning global investment power available to other funds. As he explained in a fiery speech to the European Parliament in Strasbourg that year, France was setting up a fund not to invest abroad but to protect French domestic industry from, as he put it, foreign 'predators'.[19] The fund is answerable to Parliament and invests long term in areas designed to serve the wider public interest, including support to stabilise troubled large companies. It is managed by the state-owned development bank, Caisse des Dépôts et Consignations. Sarkozy has, in effect, reversed the traditional role played by sovereign wealth funds. Instead of using it as a vehicle of overseas investment, it is designed purely for domestic support, to protect French industry and promote innovation.

The Alaskan social dividend

One of the most distinctive schemes operates in Alaska. Since 1982, the state has paid a single annual sum – a dividend – to all citizens out of the returns to the Alaskan Permanent Fund. The fund was established by referendum in 1976, and each year the state invests a quarter of its oil revenue. The original motivation was to set aside a share of the revenues from oil production for future generations of Alaskans in recognition of the inevitable depletion of the resource. Part of the petroleum asset was thereby converted into a permanent and sustainable financial asset. The fund – publicly owned by each Alaskan – is invested in a diverse portfolio and managed by a semi-independent corporation.

When the fund was initially established, there was a good deal of debate about how it should be used. While some argued that it should promote regional economic development projects, it was eventually agreed, six years later in 1982 that the returns should be used to pay a yearly dividend to current and future generations.

It is the only global example of a combined publicly owned wealth fund and a basic citizen's dividend, with the gains in the fund returned directly to the public. It combines two key principles: public ownership of wealth; and the provision of a dividend for all citizens. This is all the more significant for having been backed by the then Republican governor, Jay Hammond. The scheme is, in essence, a flat-rate cash redistribution scheme, and to some degree its genesis reflects the general distrust in the US of the state spending tax revenue to fund services. Against this, Hammond's support for the dividend payment, according to his advisers, was that it would give each citizen an individual stake in Alaska's collectively owned state wealth. 'For Hammond ... the shared core idea was neither charity, nor leveling, nor an attempt to build an income floor. [The] shared commitment was to the notion of collective ownership and the fundamental fairness of sharing the returns in equal proportion to their equal ownership.'[20]

In 2015, the fund was worth around $51 billion. The size of the dividend has fluctuated with the price of oil, the rate of return on its investment portfolio and general economic conditions, and is paid to every individual. It has varied from a high of $3,269 (in 2008) to a low of $878 in 2012. Nevertheless, an unconditional annual cash dividend of between some $3,500 and $13,000 for a family of four is significant, especially for those on the lowest incomes.

The dividend is different from a regular citizen's income in that it is an annual payment and varies in size according to the profits accruing to the Permanent Fund. Households have used the money in a variety of ways – from paying off debt and sending children to college to saving for retirement and holidays.

The scheme has been described by the academic, Karl Widerquist as 'an important and innovative example of community-owned wealth' that is converted into 'democratically distributed income'.[21] Within the state it is known as 'the third rail of Alaska politics' and is, unsurprisingly, highly popular. There is evidence that it has helped to keep a lid on the level of poverty, while easing the poverty trap and contributing to greater equality. Indeed, although other factors are at work, Alaska has the most equally distributed income among all US states, as well as the fewest households with incomes under $10,000.[22]

The Alaskan model represents the real-world application of the principle that citizens are the proper owners of the environment and have the right to share equally in its benefits. The benefits from a common asset should not be hived off to a small number of private owners. In this way, some of the economic rent relating to oil extraction has been used to benefit the whole community. There is no reason why this principle should not be applied more widely to other states and countries, using the dividends from a range of assets, including natural resources, minerals, urban land, and the electromagnetic spectrum.[23]

The Swedish wage-earner fund

One of the boldest recent examples, if short-lived, is the Swedish experiment in 'wage-earner funds', a scheme that was a good deal more radical than its sovereign wealth fund successors. This experiment began in 1983, but had its genesis in the debates in the 1970s about how to develop Sweden's social democratic model. The concept was devised in that decade in the main by Rudolf Meidner, a key architect of the Swedish welfare state and head of economics at the Swedish trade union federation. It is the only example of a social fund that has been financed by tapping privately owned assets more directly.

In Meidner's original proposal, these funds had a number of goals. They were seen, in particular, as part of a strategy to extend the social ownership of capital. Despite a highly developed welfare state, the Swedish economy at the time was still a solidly capitalist economy, with 94% of industry being privately owned. Industry itself was also highly concentrated, with around 20 corporations, many family-owned, dominating the economy, while the distribution of capital ownership was highly unequal and had hardly changed since the 1930s.

In this sense, the plan could be seen as a 'middle way' political strategy, 'to graft an element of socialism onto this capitalist productive mechanism – not the socialist propensity for planning, but its concern for social equality and well-being.'[24] Meidner also saw it as a 'step on the road towards more democratic ownership of industry and economic democracy ... as an alternative to both private capitalists and state nationalised property relations'.[25] The scheme was also seen as an important additional tool in meeting Sweden's established commitment to high levels of employment, as a way of ensuring that 'the owners of large corporations might be obliged to contribute more to the wider society without which their own profits would be impossible'.[26]

Under the original 1970s plan, all large companies would have been required to issue new shares every year, equivalent to a fifth of their profits, to be handed over to a network of regional funds.

If implemented in this form, the scheme would have been not just ambitious, but also revolutionary. The funds would have accumulated, leading to the gradual socialisation of a large part of the Swedish economy, contributing over time to greater equality in the pattern of capital ownership and the distribution of wealth, while spreading the level of industrial democracy. Under the scheme, the funds would have gradually increased their shareholding in individual companies, enabling the boards of the fund to exercise a say in company decisions. Meidner estimated that it would have taken 35 years to acquire 49% of the equity of a corporation with a profit rate of 10%.[27]

Inevitably, the plan provoked hostile opposition from employers during the 1970s, with the biggest demonstrations ever seen in Sweden at that time. Company managements were especially concerned about the ability of funds to influence company policy, and the increased role played by unions in the management of the economy. The proposal and the reaction contributed to the defeat of the ruling social democrats (SAP) in 1976 after 40 years in power.

After six years of debate, revision and ongoing controversy, the SAP won the 1982 election with a commitment to a much watered down version, a plan which was implemented 'experimentally' in 1983 and initially only for seven years. Such was the scale of business opposition, the SAP leadership in effect accepted that renewal was unlikely.[28] Instead of being required to issue new shares, the scheme charged an annual levy on wealthy shareholders, which was paid into five regional 'wage-earner investment funds'. Using a more restrictive definition of profits, only a few thousand companies were affected. The local funds were controlled and invested by local boards consisting of a range of representatives, from local trade unions to local authorities.

The levy differed from traditional corporate taxation which, as a tax on profits, subtracts from cash flow and, potentially, investment. Under the levy, the tax fell on corporate owners. In this way the value of such holdings was diluted, not the resources of corporations as a productive concern, thus, in theory, protecting capital formation.

The funds provided an income stream from capital for underwriting public spending on agreed social purposes, from pensions to socially beneficial research, thus easing pressure on wider taxation, but they also reinvested the income they yielded from dividends from the shareholdings so that they would grow over time.

The funds lasted just short of a decade. In 1992 the scheme was wound up by the incoming Conservatives, and the proceeds used to finance a string of scientific research institutes. In one sense, the great ambitions of the 1970s that had given birth to this experiment in socialisation ended in defeat. By then, the funds had grown to account for around 7% of total industrial wealth. There was also much less emphasis on industrial democracy with members of the funds appointed by the government. The ending of the scheme – which never gained widespread popular support – was certainly one of the signs of the political limits to the Swedish experiment in social democracy, though it came at a time when the Right was beginning to seize the wider intellectual ascendancy with their belief in the encouragement of free markets.[29]

Yet while the Swedish scheme enjoyed only limited success, it does have important lessons. Financing a fund through a direct charge on capital has the effect of transferring, over time, a proportion of privately owned wealth into a collectively owned asset. It is a device that offers a direct way of limiting the private ownership of capital and ensuring that some of the gains from ownership are more equally shared. The idea might sound radical in a UK context, but it is an idea that, as shown in Chapter Six, was first proposed by a distinguished UK economist well before a variant was adopted by Sweden.

FIVE

How to pay for the UK's first social wealth fund

Although the UK has yet to establish its own social wealth fund, a political debate about their merits has finally emerged, and there is now an overwhelming economic and social case for establishing one or more such funds. The adoption of one or more schemes would contribute to the tackling of some of the most pressing faultlines in the British economic and social model, helping to correct, in particular, for the problem of the overdominance of private capital.

Such funds offer an alternative to old-style public ownership. They would also reintroduce an element of longer-term planning into economic and social policy, better able to deal with longer-term needs and changes. This is a crucial element of social management that has been greatly weakened in recent times, with key decisions on public spending and social provision increasingly being subject to political expediency.

Of course, some variants are much more radical than others. But there are no overriding political reasons why the UK should not follow the lead of other countries with its own model scheme. Indeed, the principle has been set. The UK has already established such a fund, albeit a temporary one – UK Financial Investments. This was set up in November 2008 to manage HM Treasury's shareholdings in a number of banks, a refinancing deal necessary to prevent widespread banking failure. The fund is managed by an arm's length quango, was worth around £30 billion in 2014 and could have been used to establish a fledgling social fund, yet the government's plan is to sell the shares and eventually to close the fund.[1]

The international examples as examined in Chapter Four have nearly all been funded by two distinct sources of finance. The Swedish wage-earner fund was financed by an annual private levy on capital. Most sovereign wealth funds, in contrast, have been financed by the use of part of the income from the exploitation of natural resources, mostly oil.

There are several alternative potential sources of funding for one or more UK funds:

- First, from the returns from the better management of existing public wealth, including where appropriate, the proceeds from the sale of public assets. Despite three decades of sell-offs, large chunks of wealth in the UK – from land and buildings to infrastructure – remain publicly owned.
- Second, from the public revenue from the use of natural resources including oil, gas and land. The UK is, of course, late to this game and has lost a large part of the historic opportunity that came with the proceeds of North Sea oil, but there will be a continuing, if shallower and slowing, flow of revenue from this source.
- Third, from the redirection of the proceeds of some existing taxation or the establishment of new taxation. At the moment, the proceeds from those taxes aimed at least in part at socialising unearned gains – such as capital gains tax, inheritance tax and some property taxes – are paid into the general tax pool, mixed in with all other tax receipts. Instead, such receipts could be paid into relevant social wealth funds.
- A final possibility would be to use private levies such as a direct charge on company profits or on share ownership, or tapping some of the revenue from certain forms of financial transaction that involve an element of economic rent.

A key principle inherent to such funds is that of hypothecation, with the proceeds of particular taxes or public actions being earmarked for specific purposes. This is the principle that underpins the funding of the BBC through the television licence. In a more recent example, the government is to introduce a new levy on large employers (at 0.5% of payroll) to counter the low level of workplace training by paying for a rise in the number of apprenticeships.[2] Making the announcement, the Chancellor commentated that: 'there are too many large companies who … take a free ride on the system', an explicit recognition of the extent of market failure on training.[3]

One advantage of hypothecation is that the means by which certain types of investment and social provision are financed would immediately be recognised by the public. Such greater clarity would help to promote the merits of such funds and, where financed in this way, the taxation shifts they would involve. Indeed, there is evidence that, by making the link between funding and outcome explicit, hypothecation gains public support in a way which generic taxation does not.[4]

Table 5.1 outlines four possible funds: a public ownership fund; a public investment and social fund; a social housing fund; and a social care fund. The starting point for a UK social wealth fund should be the establishment of a public ownership fund. This could be created from the pooling of all Britain's existing publicly owned assets. Such a fund would be distinct from the other funds, in that it would hold and accumulate public physical capital and assets and disburse the investment income from the use of that capital. The other funds outlined in Table 5.1 are, in essence, deposit accounts for hypothecated taxes and charges to be invested and redistributed for social purposes.

A public ownership fund

Despite three decades of sell-offs, the public sector is still a substantial asset holder. Such assets – worth together at least £1.2 trillion – include land, public sector housing, office buildings, schools and hospitals,

Table 5.1: Potential social wealth funds, UK

Fund	Possible sources of funding	Purpose
Public ownership fund	Created from the pooling of existing public sector assets into a single fund, managed by independent financial experts to secure improved returns. The fund and its returns could be a central source of the funding for a new public investment and social fund.	To preserve and grow the public asset base and ensure that the rewards of such common ownership are shared across society.
Public investment and social fund	The income from the better management of public assets through a public ownership fund (as above). The tax revenue from North Sea oil and the development of other natural resources. The proceeds from the use of other common assets, such as the sale of the electromagnetic spectrum. Windfall taxes. A levy on some forms of financial activity such as acquisitions and mergers.	To help boost the rate of private and public investment, improve the quality of economic and social infrastructure and support existing and new social programmes aimed at improving social opportunities.
Social housing fund	The revenue from the sales of social housing. Some existing taxes on housing such as stamp duty. The introduction of a new tax on development gain, such as a land value tax, or through the proceeds from a community-owned land bank. (Alternatively, the proceeds from these sources could be paid into the public investment and social fund).	To boost the volume of social housing.
Social care fund	From the introduction of higher property taxes, such as a capital gains tax on first homes Or an enhanced inheritance tax.	To boost the quality of social care.

forestry land, equipment and most of the transport network, including land around railway stations.[5]

Some of these assets, especially those held in land and property, have significant commercial potential. Organisations that have large surplus or undeveloped land holdings include Network Rail, the NHS, the Ministry of Defence, a plethora of other government departments and local government.

As Lord Adonis, a former Labour minister and head of the National Infrastructure Commission, launched in 2015, has pointed out, the London boroughs own between a quarter and a third of land within their boundaries, most of it within housing estates, much of it undeveloped. Transport for London owns 5,800 acres of land, an area larger than the entire London Borough of Camden, much of it in prime locations.[6]

There is a very strong case for pooling Britain's publicly owned wealth into a single protected social wealth fund – a public ownership fund. Britain, along with most other nations with large public sector holdings, has a woeful record on managing such assets. In 2011, for example, the coalition government announced that it wanted to dispose of enough land in four years to build 100,000 homes. But according to the Public Accounts Committee, no record had been kept of homes built or sale proceeds. The committee described the government's approach as 'wishful thinking dressed up as public policy' and concluded:

> The Department for Communities and Local Government cannot demonstrate the success of the land disposal programme in addressing the housing shortage or achieving value for money, because it does not collect information on the actual number of houses built or under construction, the proceeds from land sold, or whether the parcels of land were sold at market value …[7]

For the most part, the UK's stock of public assets is poorly recorded. If such national assets were better identified and managed, they have the potential to generate significant commercial returns that could be used for the public good. The best way of achieving better management and returns would be to transfer all public assets to a national or series of local Public Ownership Funds. This could mobilise assets that already exist. Since the UK has depleted much of its mineral wealth and has the opposite of a trade surplus, this would be a primary source for creating the country's first social wealth fund.

The Organisation for Economic Co-operation and Development (OECD) has drawn up international guidelines for the better management of state-owned assets.[8] The pooling of such assets has been strongly advocated by the leading Swedish public sector reformers Dag Detter and Stefan Fölster. Both have been involved in improving the management of public wealth in Sweden, and argue that all countries should pool their public assets to be run by holding companies with considerable political independence and power. These would be managed by professional managers in a transparent way and shielded from political interference. The aim would be to deliver maximum public gain, with the respective economic and social goals clearly laid out: 'Putting state-owned commercial assets into an independent ring-fenced holding company at arm's length from short-term political interference and with professional management brings strategic and financial expertise and advantages to the operations as well as economic benefits to the country.'[9]

Such political outsourcing would, in some respects, replicate the way in which public sector pension schemes are managed, by independent boards free of political control, and would mirror, in some ways, Labour's 1997 decision to transfer political control over interest rates to an independent Bank of England.

Several countries have already experimented with such an approach, though with mixed results and mixed levels of independence. Perhaps the best-known example of such pooling is in Singapore, which first established such a holding company, Temasek Holdings, in 1974. Today it manages all state-owned commercial assets apart from large holdings in property, while its social and economic objectives are set out clearly in its charter. It is worth more than half the country's GDP. Although Temasek has attracted some ongoing political controversy, largely on how independent from government it really is, it has become a role model for a number of other countries and it boasts an impressive average annual return of 17%, which is above that achieved in the private sector.

In mid-2015, 16 countries, including Malaysia, Vietnam, Dubai, Austria and Finland, operated such national wealth funds formed from the pooling of public assets. These are concentrated in Asia and the Middle East. Together they have an aggregate value of some US$1.1 trillion, though this still represents only a tiny fraction of global public assets.[10] Austria's Fund, ÖIAG, has performed better than the Austrian stock market index, ATX, since it was established in the 1970s, and pays considerable annual dividends to the Austrian government. Although it is still early to evaluate their success, Finland created Solidium in 2008 and Vietnam created SCIC in 2005.

Such national wealth funds are distinct from sovereign wealth funds and some countries, including Singapore, have both. National wealth funds manage actual physical assets, while sovereign wealth funds are essentially fund managers which invest portfolios of cash, mainly in overseas equities and companies.

In essence, national wealth funds offer governments a third way between nationalisation and privatisation, with assets staying in common ownership and with the dividends from their use being retained by the state. They provide a way of consolidating and growing publicly owned wealth, without the gains accruing elsewhere. They are, as Detter and Fölster have put it:

> the perfect compromise: they keep public assets under government ownership while simultaneously preventing undue government interference. The state appoints the auditors and the board responsible for the portfolio, and decides which assets should be sold when sufficiently developed, but it cannot influence how the fund itself is managed.[11]

Although some of the assets could be sold, the revenue from sales would, unlike the current practice of privatisation, be retained by the fund. The returns from improved management could be used in two distinct ways: part could be reinvested to enable the fund to grow over time, while part could be used to finance agreed projects. There is a clear logic to using the returns from public wealth for reinvestment – these are assets paid for and developed on behalf of the public over many years, sometimes generations.

Of course, there are important practical questions: on how long it would take to establish a complete record of such assets, on how such a fund should be managed, about the degree of independence from government, and on what sort of investment criteria and methods should be deployed.

- Should all assets be included, or some, such as the social housing stock, be held in a separate fund?
- Should the state set the broad objectives of such funds, and then hand over detailed management to an independent board, or should it retain a hands-on role?
- What about the question of the mix between social and commercial criteria in determining investment? Should the aim be solely to maximise financial returns, or should social goals be built into the investment strategy?
- What about investing overseas?
- What issues might be raised about the commercial exploitation of certain public assets such as public parks or forestry land?
- What form should the management boards take and who appoints them?
- Is there a risk that such funds might succumb to the same kind of short-termism that afflicts the private sector?
- How can an ever hungry Treasury be kept at arm's length, especially during periods of economic turbulence?

In 2015, for example, there were fears, never in fact realised, that the Chancellor might be seeking to raid the National Lottery Fund as part of the autumn spending review.[12]

Of course, similar issues apply equally to other forms of social wealth fund that involve an element of investment.

To date, successive British governments have chosen a quite different and highly questionable route for the management of publicly owned assets. Since the beginning of the 1980s, over £200 billion worth of former nationalised industries and utilities, from British Gas to Eurostar, along with a swathe of public land and buildings have been sold.[13] Many of these have been sold at a considerable loss. The first chunk of Royal Mail shares sold in 2015 could have realised an additional £1 billion, while a report by the National Audit Office found that taxpayers had invested four times more in Eurostar, approximately £3 billion, than the sum recouped from the company's sale in March 2015.[14]

In addition, around three million homes have been sold under the 'Right to Buy' scheme, equivalent to some £200 billion in today's values. Whatever the merits of particular privatisations, and these have been and will continue to be hotly debated, there is little justification for the proceeds to go lock, stock and barrel into the Treasury black hole.

The state is, in effect, the custodian of such assets, which have mostly been accumulated over long periods of time with taxpayers' money. Public assets are, like natural assets, part of the common wealth, owned collectively by all citizens. Selling them to private owners may land a short-term revenue hit for the government, enabling them to cut taxes or reduce national debt, but at the expense of a substantial dilution in the collectively owned asset base and of that available to future generations.

Together with the revenue from North Sea oil, much of Britain's social and industrial heritage – the family silver – has gone, sold at a discount, largely in ways that have benefited the few, intensifying the overall concentration of wealth and further enhancing the role of private capital in the economy. This adds up to a significant failure of economic and social management by successive governments. The last 30 years have witnessed the application of short-sighted economics, driven by an obsession with immediate political gain – jam today, an approach which parallels much of the blatant short-termism endemic to big business.

The privatisation juggernaut was originally sold by Mrs Thatcher as the route to the much vaunted 'popular capitalism'. Yet this has always been a myth. Shares bought by the public through privatisation have mostly been sold immediately, while share ownership is even more concentrated today than in the 1980s.

A large number of privatised companies have been bought up by private equity groups, and are thus no longer even public listed companies. Out of the 23 privatised local and regional water companies, ten are now foreign owned, with a further eight bought by private equity.[15] In most of these cases, the company finances have been engineered, largely through the use of leveraged debt, to maximise the gain to investors at the expense of other players, including employees, consumers and taxpayers.[16]

It is a similar story across other privatised sectors – from the railways to care homes. The fixation with private ownership is also now increasingly out of step with other countries which have been unwinding their own privatisation programmes, including taking water services back into a form of public ownership in response to the way the utilities have been exploited for private gain.[17]

In his first post-election budget in July 2015, George Osborne announced that he intended to sell a further £32 billion worth of state assets – from Lloyds Bank and RBS to the Green Investment Bank and the Student Loan Book – in 2015/16 alone, and a total of over £60 billion by the end of the Parliament.[18] In an attempt to boost the pace of selling still further, local authorities have been told they can keep the proceeds of sales of local assets from parks and swimming pools to libraries. Some of these national sales, including the return of RBS to the private sector, will involve a considerable loss to the taxpayer. No longer able to claim that it will spread popular capitalism, and spread wealth, the government has a new defence: that sales will help to pay down the deficit.

Yet it makes little sense to use long-term capital assets to finance a temporary revenue gap. Sales offer a one-off windfall – the family silver can only be sold once. They mean the permanent loss of collectively owned public assets and the income that they deliver over time, both built up over many decades. Although such sales can reduce the cash debt at a given moment – the government's argument – they aggravate the problem of public indebtedness as the asset base which helps to balance the debt shrinks away. As the Oxford economist John Muellbauer has argued, instead of concentrating on debt alone, governments should 'target the growth of better-measured government debt minus government assets, all relative to national income. Increasing government gross debt would then not be a concern if it was matched by an increase in assets, such as publicly-owned productive infrastructure and land.'[19]

A public ownership fund, created by pooling all assets into a single, independently managed fund, would end this short-termism. Such assets could, after public debate, still be sold, but the revenue from such sales would be retained in the fund. This means that the collective asset base would be maintained. Over time, the fund would accumulate in value through a mix of sales revenue and investment dividends.

In this way, the benefits of historically accumulated public assets could be used to fund economic and social projects that benefit society as a whole. If such a fund had been created at the beginning of the great public sell-off, it would have funded a higher level of investment at a lower level of public borrowing, building the productive base and contributing to the creation of a much more robust and resilient economy.

Such a public ownership fund could stand alone and be managed separately from other social wealth funds, becoming over time a substantial source of funding for the public good. Alternatively, a public ownership fund could be incorporated into a distinct public investment and social fund and thus be a substantial source of revenue for its goals.

A public investment and social fund

A public investment and social fund would pay for a boost to public investment in infrastructure and urban renewal – from transport facilities to new schools – and help pay for certain kinds of private investment. It could also help to fund new social programmes. A public investment and social fund could use its revenue to invest in other assets, including equities and property, and thus be allowed to grow over time. By taking equity stakes in other companies, some of the gains accruing from corporate success would be democratised and shared for wider social use without direct public ownership.

If the public ownership fund was incorporated into the public investment and social fund, much of its funding would come directly from this source. But it could also be funded in other, additional ways. In this sense it would be part-funded by managing capital assets, in part from other revenue streams deposited in the fund and in some cases through share transfers.

One additional source could be the revenue from resource exploitation, including the remaining tax revenue from North Sea oil, though the revenue flow will be affected by the 2015 fall in the price of oil. Though the oil will run out at some point, it is estimated that up to a further 16 billion extractable barrels are left. A public investment and social fund could also draw on the revenue from the exploitation of other common assets, such as the electromagnetic spectrum.

Another possibility would be a small charge on merger and acquisition activity, paid by the transfer of share holdings of the resulting company. Much of this activity, which is mostly conducted at inflated values, provides a form of rentier income to a small group of executives and financiers organising the deals, and a tax would extract some of these gains. With payment in shares, some of the future gains enjoyed through dividend payments will accrue to wider society.

The occasional one-off taxes on windfall profits, such as those levied in the past on banks, energy companies and oil producers, could also be paid into such a fund in the form of shares. In 1981, for example, the then-chancellor Geoffrey Howe introduced a special budget levy of around £400 million on the banks, which were seen to be escaping the pain of the then recession. This sum constituted around a fifth of their profits in that year. In 1982, the Treasury sought to share the benefit of high oil prices, by imposing a special tax on North Sea oil and gas, which raised £2.4 billion. Then in 1997, the incoming Labour government imposed a windfall tax of some £5 billion on the 'excess profits'[20] of the privatised utilities, including BAA, British Gas, British Telecom and Powergen. The proceeds were used to fund a new welfare-to-work scheme, designed to help the young and long-term unemployed back into work.

In December 2009, the Chancellor, Alistair Darling, announced a new bank payroll tax: 'a special one-off levy of 50 per cent on any individual discretionary bonus above £25,000' to be paid by the bank, not the bank employee. The levy raised some £3.5 billion in gross terms in 2010/11.[21]

A similar proposal, for a 'national community fund' has been suggested by Gerald Holtham, former director of the left-of-centre Institute for Public Policy Research (IPPR), and now an adviser to the Welsh finance minister. Holtham argues that such a fund should be managed by commercial managers to help provide additional funding for Britain's public services.[22] It could, he suggests, be financed in a variety of ways, including by hypothecating revenue from the sale of state assets, from land sales and from telecommunication auctions.

Holtham also proposes a scrip tax on certain corporate transactions, paid in shares not cash. These would dilute existing shareholdings but result in no cash outflow or liquidity strain on the company. He also suggests that instead of buying gilt-edged securities, which have largely benefited the richest members of society, further rounds of quantitative easing should be used to buy equities to place in the fund. This would fit with the growing debate about the need for a shift in the nature of monetary policy with governments taking more direct responsibility to create money and inject it into the real economy, though most proposals have suggested channeling the additional credit either into investment in infrastructure or via direct payments to citizens. The latter approach is often dubbed 'helicopter money' and was first advocated by the pro-market economist and Nobel Laureate, Milton Friedman in 1969.[23]

One of those who has called for just such a shift is Lord Adair Turner, former chairman of the now abolished Financial Services Authority.

As he puts it, '… compared with a pure monetary stimulus [such as quantitative easing], it works through putting new spending power directly into the hands of a broad swathe of households and businesses, rather than working through the indirect transmission mechanism of higher asset prices and induced private sector credit expansion'.[24]

Some of these funding options could generate substantial revenue. If the £350 billion quantitative easing programme had been used in this way, Holtham estimates that such a fund would now be 'worth over a fifth of annual GDP'.[25] In 2015, UK merger and acquisition deals, such as the £47 billion takeover of gas explorer BG Group by oil giant Royal Dutch Shell, were heading for a total of some £400 billion, the highest level since 2008.[26] Even a modest scrip tax of, say, 2% would generate up to £8 billion worth of shares into a fund over the year. The sale of the 4G spectrum in 2013 raised £2.3 billion, while Ofcom has estimated that the 5G spectrum, expected to be ready for auction in 2018, is likely to be much larger.

Such a fund would operate a little bit like the national lottery, though with a variety of funding sources. The annual revenue from the management of the fund could be used for a number of purposes that benefit the wider public, including boosting public investment and providing funding for a range of proven social programmes.

The UK has a poor record on investment, private and public, over recent decades. The quality and volume of social housing, transport, education and broadband is mostly below the standard needed for an advanced economy. The level of public sector investment as a share of GDP is set to fall to 1.5%, well below the average of almost 5% achieved between 1948 and the mid-1970s and even the 3.2% level in 2009/10.[27] The OECD says that developed economies should spend a minimum of 3.5% of GDP on infrastructure. The World Economic Forum ranked the UK 24th for 'quality of overall infrastructure' in its 2012 report on global competitiveness.[28] In addition, innovation rates and research and development spending have been internationally low, well below the EU average.[29] In setting up a National Infrastructure Commission, the government acknowledges this problem, but has yet to identify the resources to make it work, intent it seems to rely on overseas funding, and thus ownership, for major structural projects.

There is now a growing acceptance that the state should play a bigger role in raising investment levels, public and private, and, as is commonplace in many countries, should have a central investment function. It is hardly a new idea. As Adam Smith argued in the *Wealth of Nations*, published in 1776, the state has a responsibility for the 'erection and maintenance' of those 'public works and institutions' which, while of great advantage to society, would not profit private enterprise.[30]

Although it should be a key part of their economic role, corporate capitalism and the financial services industry have, in recent decades, proved poor mechanisms for ensuring an adequate flow of funds for private investment. While the finance sector has, over time, helped to facilitate entrepreneurship and promote investment and trade, this primary role has become increasingly marginal in recent decades. Instead, the lion's share of financial investment has gone into property, which has simply inflated the price of existing homes, increased the household debt burden, and undermined the productive base of the economy. This has been a central factor in rising economic instability and is one of the main reasons for Britain's low level of productivity growth and innovation and increasingly low-paid economy. The state has also fallen short in its responsibilities for building and maintaining both infrastructure and social capital. A public investment and social fund would aim to help correct both these private and public sector deficiencies. If it was independently managed, the public investment and social fund would not be vulnerable to political interference or a Treasury grab.

Such a fund could also be used to help support a British state investment bank, aimed at raising the investment rate and improving finance, particularly long-term financing, for small and medium-sized businesses.[31] Such a bank could also be used to secure some of the benefits from state-supported innovation. Too often, governments have failed to take a stake in new technology that they have helped to foster, leaving all the gains to private investors.

Like social wealth funds, such banks are widely used elsewhere. There is a European Investment Bank, a Nordic Investment Bank, and a number of others, all established to aid the financing of government-mandated projects by borrowing in the capital markets.

The UK already has a Green Investment Bank, launched in 2012 with £3.8 billion of public sector money for investment in energy efficiency projects and a key source of patient finance. Although the Bank became profitable in 2014, the government – in a highly controversial move- plans to sell a majority stake to the private sector, so that private sector companies will control the entire portfolio. It is a move that has been widely condemned, not least by leading Conservatives including Ben Goldsmith, brother of MP Zac Goldsmith and chairman of the Conservative Environment Network. Ben Caldecott, associate fellow of the Conservative pressure group Bright Blue, said that 'the last thing we need is a publicly supported, but privately owned, asset manager using subsidised capital and jobs to compete with the private sector'.[32]

Over time, a public investment and social fund could grow its financial strength and help to grow productive capacity and could also boost social capital. Social projects could be targeted at disadvantaged communities and raising social mobility, with greater help being given to proven existing and new projects. By filling the gaps left by markets and traditional public sector activity, these could improve educational, training and life opportunities among the poorest. These might include loan funding to social enterprises and local charitable organisations, schemes aimed at job creation in unemployment hot spots, and improved training opportunities and funding to support the local youth services that have been so heavily cut back in the post-2010 austerity drive. Such funding could also be used to reinstate the educational maintenance grants for poorer 16–18 year olds to stay on in further education; these were scrapped in the first round of the post-2010 public spending cuts.

The fund could also help to raise the number of educational bursaries and scholarships in areas of low participation. Currently, fewer than one in 25 from the poorest areas reach top universities, and there has been little improvement over the last 15 years. Inequalities between school achievement rates are a significant factor in the lack of opportunities among the poorest. Although most universities offer scholarships – a proven route for encouraging upward social mobility – these are greatly oversubscribed. The educational charity the Sutton Trust has proposed a US-style per cent scheme, which would nurture able children from disadvantaged backgrounds to the point where they could meet the elite institutions' entry requirements. Such a scheme would aim at helping those from poorer backgrounds to compete on equal terms and thereby widen access to the most competitive courses.[33]

A social housing fund and a social care fund

Separate social wealth funds could also be established to help to address two of today's most deep-seated social problems: Britain's dysfunctional housing market and the serious underfunding of social care.

There is now a growing housing crisis. The problems of homelessness and overcrowding, the rising cost of housing and deteriorating access have all been exacerbated by the steep decline of social housebuilding, three decades of the Right to Buy and an overreliance on the private market.

Since it was introduced in the early 1980s, the ongoing sell-off of council homes has contributed to the shrinking of the stock of social housing, and from the outset, local authorities have been largely prevented from using the proceeds to build replacement houses. Right to Buy has transferred a large proportion of communally owned assets into private hands, though initially to those with low levels of existing wealth. This has increased the wealth holdings of those buying, but has depleted the stock of social housing at the expense of those now unable to get onto the social housing ladder. The opportunities of one generation have been enhanced at the expense of another.

Instead of this approach, the revenues from sales could have been pooled to create local *social housing funds* to be used to finance replacement social building. The government is now extending the Right to Buy, again at significant discounts, to housing association tenants. This proposal has proved highly controversial. It will further deplete the already shrinking number of affordable rented homes, while threatening the long-held independence of housing associations and the future of some 2.5 million social homes. Formerly private housing associations are being reclassified as public sector bodies, making them much more vulnerable to wholesale privatisation, adding to the likelihood that we are heading even closer to the end of social housing.

Today, the proceeds from all public and social housing sales should be paid directly into local social housing funds. Such funds could also be boosted by the revenue from some existing property taxes, including stamp duty, or from new taxes on the development gain from land, or from public land banks, and used to boost the provision of social housing for rent.

In a similar way, a social care fund could be created to help provide additional finance to meet the escalating cost of social care. Because of growing longevity, social care is big business in the UK. Yet such care is increasingly privately provided and paid for (more than 60% of care home residents pay in full or in part for their care), while the chance and cost of decent care in old age has become more and more of a lottery. In the year to April 2015, the Care Quality Commission found high levels of inadequacy across adult social care services, including residential care.[34]

How to manage social care is one of the biggest social issues facing the country, yet successive governments have ducked the issue time and again. Some have their care paid for by the state, depending on their level of individual savings, but those above the savings limit pay for it through their own assets and wealth. The present Conservative government had promised to impose a cap on this individual contribution for residential care bills (of £72,000) as recommended by the 2011 Dilnot Commission, as a way of limiting what are often staggering bills.[35] But the government is now to delay this plan until 2020.

The cap is not without its critics. One of its key effects is that a greater proportion of the costs of social care would be transferred from individuals to taxpayers. Poorer, younger sections of society would be paying some of the social care costs of better-off pensioners with that saving passed on to their heirs. Intergenerational fairness requires that those with sufficient wealth use a greater proportion of it to fund their social care, thus sharing the burden more equitably between those receiving care – and their children – and younger taxpayers. As two critics of the cap have argued, the cap would 'preserve individual wealth and, in practice housing wealth, at the expense of the public purse. Ultimately, it will benefit those who will inherit that wealth. The use of public funds to preserve an inheritance lies at the heart of our criticism.'[36]

There is a strong fairness and intergenerational argument for tapping into personal wealth to fund social care (or other social provision) by requiring homeowners to use at least part of their wealth in their lifetime, rather than passing on most or all to their heirs. Because of soaring house prices and the extension of home ownership, housing wealth is by far the largest element in personal disposable assets and is very unequally distributed. Property wealth accounts for 39% of the total level of personal wealth of some £9.5 trillion, while financial wealth (including share holdings and savings) accounts for 11%.[37] On average, long-standing property owners have enjoyed substantial gains, a large part unearned, yet main residences are exempt from capital gains tax, while the level of inheritance tax paid on wealth above a certain limit has been significantly eroded over time.

One way of tackling the problem of social care and its underfunding so that the burden is shared more equally would be through a new and explicit 'social care tax' on housing wealth, with the proceeds paid into a new social care fund. Such a tax could be justified as a way of redistributing part of the unearned gains from home ownership to use exclusively for social care. In this way, the taxpayer's contribution to social care would be explicit and transparent, while the cost of current care would not become an excessive burden on younger taxpayers.

A ring-fenced social care fund financed by such a tax (and which paid for part of the national care bill) might be much easier to sell to homeowners who have long been protective of their wealth and their ability to pass it on to their children. There is, of course, a short-term as well as a long-term issue here. Extra social care funding is needed now. Whether a fund could finance extra care now and be allowed to grow or would have to be fully spent each year would depend on the scale of the revenue received.

Such an idea has been gathering some support. It was one of the recommendations from a panel discussion on the theme of 'The Unequal State', organised by the British-based Royal Society of Arts, at the 2015 European Forum held in the Austrian village, Alpbach. The panel argued for 'creating a wealth fund funded from housing values of seniors to the state in exchange for more social care'.[38]

The principle of funding care through capital taxation is also gaining support. In 2014, the Commission on the Future of Health and Social Care in England, set up by the health think tank the King's Fund and chaired by the economist Kate Barker, suggested that extra funding for social care should come from a revision of capital taxation, especially property taxation. The possibilities examined included an end-of-life tax on capital gains, extending capital gains tax to primary residences, a higher inheritance tax, a flat-rate charge (at £20,000), or levying a percentage charge on wealth at the point of state pension age. The commission suggested that such payments could be made as a lump sum, in instalments, or at death. The commission argued that 'the case for applying capital gains tax to housing is powerful', while also acknowledging the political constraints.[39]

This is undoubtedly a politically sensitive area. In 2010, increasingly bitter cross-party talks on the issue had broken down, in part over a proposal by the then Labour government for a 10% levy on inheritance to pay for social care. Despite its merits, the proposal was soon attacked by sections of the media and political opponents. The *Daily Mail* dubbed it: 'Labour's secret plan for a 10% death tax raid on the estates of Middle Britain'.[40] During the 2010 election campaign, the Conservatives used a poster depicting a gravestone engraved with 'RIP Off', and the message: 'Now Gordon wants £20,000 when you die'.

Whatever the case for implementing a targeted social care tax based on inheritance, it is time to review the whole question of how to tax wealth and inheritance. As Geoff Mulgan, former Director of

Policy at 10 Downing Street under Tony Blair, has argued: 'Perhaps the biggest social issue of the next decade [is] how to achieve a fundamental redistribution of assets to reverse the recent shift towards more unequal wealth.'[41]

If this is to be achieved, there will need to be an increase in the share of the total tax-take coming from wealth. As shown in Table 5.2, taxes on property and wealth (including council tax) contribute only 7% of all tax revenue (one of the lowest rates among rich nations), compared with 60% from income tax, national insurance contributions and VAT. Inheritance tax and capital gains tax provide only 1.2% of all revenue, and stamp duty on shares only 0.4%. The estimated £9.5 trillion in property and other assets owned by private households in the UK is very unevenly distributed and attracts a relatively low level of taxation.[42]

Table 5.2: Tax revenue by source, 2012/13

	% of total receipts
Income tax	25.9
NICs	17.5
VAT	17.0
Corporation tax	6.7
Fuel duties	4.4
Business rates	4.3
Alcohol and tobacco duties	3.4
Property and wealth taxes	7.0
Council tax	4.4
Stamp duty land tax	1.1
Inheritance tax	0.5
Capital gains tax	0.6
Stamp duty on shares	0.4
Other taxes and receipts	13.7

Source: K Lawton and H Reed, *Property and Wealth Taxes in the UK*, London, IPPR, 2013, Table 1.1

In the 1930s, nearly a third of deaths resulted in death duties; this is down to just 3% today.[43] The inheritance tax system is full of loopholes and exemptions, which allow many of the richest to avoid any tax at all on the passing on of family wealth. By 2020, couples may, depending on their circumstances, be able to pass on as much £1 million of their estate free of inheritance tax, noticeably more than at the moment.

Is it right that large chunks of private capital, much of which has already been passed down through history and is unearned even by those who have accumulated it, should be passed down to family members who played little to no role in producing it? This is even more questionable when much of this wealth stems less from personal effort and risk-taking than from societal norms and community social and economic decisions. The inheritance of such wealth is a significant factor in the opportunity gap of each generation.

There is a strong case for taxing wealth more heavily, including a higher proportion of wealth that is passed on. This would be one way of expanding a tax base that has been slowly shrinking over time and would mean more people paying and at a higher rate. Further, using the revenue in clearly targeted ways – such as to pay into a social care fund – might make such additional taxation more politically saleable.

SIX

Power cut: the dilution of capital ownership and a citizen's payment

The proposals mentioned earlier – to establish funds that help to finance additional public investment, new homes and better social care – would rely on a mix of three main types of funding:

- the revenue from the management of publicly owned assets;
- the revenue from existing and new forms of progressive taxation;
- the revenue from new charges on some forms of corporate activity.

New restrictions on the sales of public assets would limit the growth of private capital. A much more radical approach would be to adapt the Swedish wage-earner fund model (see Chapter Four), by securing additional revenue directly from the dilution of existing capital ownership. Requiring companies to issue new shares that diluted existing share ownership, or levying an annual charge on existing shareholding, would allow for the socialisation over time of part of the privately owned stock of capital. Such a charge would present a more direct challenge to capitalism's inbuilt tendency to ever-widening inequality.

Such a levy (additional to the current stamp duty of 0.5% on the purchase of shares) would be a hypothecated tax on that part of wealth held in the form of shares, and would be one way of ensuring that the gains from growing prosperity were more equally shared than they have been over the last three decades. As shown in Table 2.1 in Chapter Two, most UK shareholdings – almost 54% – are owned by institutions and individuals from outside the UK. This proportion has risen from 8% in 1963 to 31% in 1998 and 43% in 2010, a huge jump in the internationalisation of corporate ownership. Of shares owned abroad, nearly half are held in the United States. Those held domestically are predominantly owned by institutions – including insurance companies, banks and other financial institutions and pension funds. Only 12% are owned by individuals (including company directors) heavily concentrated among higher income groups, with financial assets the most unequally distributed of all personal wealth.

Such a levy could either help to provide additional finance for the proposed public investment and social fund or be used to fund a quite separate collectively owned unit trust and used for other purposes.

James Meade and Labour's 'National Workers' Capital Fund'

Significantly, although such a scheme was implemented in Sweden, the origins of this idea lie with the distinguished British economist and Nobel Laureate James Meade. Meade had worked with Keynes and was an adviser to the Wilson governments from the 1960s, and later the Social Democratic Party (SDP)/Liberal Alliance. He had long been concerned with the question of inequality and the need, as he described it, to 'increase the amount of property that was in social ownership'.[1]

In 1965, he published a short book, *Efficiency, Equality and the Ownership of Property*. This addressed a specific issue: the impact of accelerated automation on the workforce. Meade argued that this would increase the return to capital and lower the wage share, thus intensifying the extent of inequality, while ushering in an age of much greater insecurity among the workforce. In this he was remarkably prescient, anticipating a number of future trends in the jobs market, including the fall in the wage share, though automation is only one of a number of explanations for this trend.[2]

Technological change in recent decades has certainly contributed to a continuing upheaval in pay, jobs and opportunities, while many argue that we are now facing a significant acceleration in this process. The march of automation, along with other deep-seated economic trends, has already had a significant impact on work opportunities in recent years. Since the mid-1970s, the British economy has been running at a higher level of unemployment than in the immediate post-war era, some of it driven by the way technology has been eliminating a range of jobs, not just those involving routine tasks but also many middle-paying and middle-skill jobs, a process that economists have labelled 'the hollowing out of the middle'.

The potential threat to jobs and opportunities posed by the impact of automation – with machines replacing human beings – is hardly new. In the early 1950s, it is said that Henry Ford II was showing the automobile trade union leader, Walter Reuther, around one of his new state-of-the-art factories in Detroit. Ford halted at one of the new robots and asked Reuther how he could get them to join his union? Quick as a flash came the reply: 'And how are you going to get them to buy your cars?' At the time, Detroit was a thriving metropolis, bustling with energy, with a big and growing middle class. Today it is a burnt-out city, a symbol of the destructive winds of change that have swept through the US, leading to the collapse of livelihoods, destroyed by what some have dubbed the four horsemen of the apocalypse: technical change, globalisation, the free market and the end of collective bargaining.

Today, many argue that the threat posed by automation is rising sharply. We are on the edge of a new age of 3-D printing, driverless cars, delivery drones, and ever cleverer robots that can write newspaper articles, cook and serve fast food, stock shelves and make beds. A spate of recent books – from Erik Brynjolfsson's *The Second Machine Age* to *The Rise of the Robots* by Martin Ford – predict that the backwash from the new automation earthquake has only just begun.

Brynjolfsson, Ford and others argue that today's upheaval could be much more embracing than the agricultural and industrial revolutions.[3] The risk is to a much wider range of jobs – high-paid lawyers, middle and senior managers, drivers, distribution and warehouse workers alike. 'Automation,' as one commentator has put it, 'is blind to the colour of your collar'.[4]

There is a real risk that, without strong counteracting measures, continued globalisation and de-unionisation will, along with automation, create societies ever more polarised between wealth and impoverishment. The conservative American economist Tyler Cowen suggests that, with the continuing erosion of middle-paid jobs, we are facing an ever deeper division between 'broken communities and extreme affluence'.[5] Martin Ford, a Silicon Valley entrepreneur, puts the risk rather more colourfully: 'the plutocracy [might] shut itself away in gated communities or in elite cities, perhaps guarded by autonomous military robots and drones'.[6]

Over fifty years ago, Meade set out a number of potential solutions to the risk of ever-growing inequality, notably through two broad strategies aimed at securing a more equal distribution of private ownership:

- First, through higher taxation on wealth and inheritance aimed at breaking down large concentrations of wealth, the solution later advocated by Thomas Piketty.[7]
- Second, and more radically, he advocated measures aimed at increasing the level of social ownership of capital by using the state to build a growing stake in national wealth. Importantly, he linked this scheme to providing the finance to 'pay out an equal social dividend to each citizen'.[8]

Both sets of measures were to supplement, not replace, existing mechanisms of the welfare state.

What Meade had in mind was a more evenly based 'property-owning democracy', though a very different vision from Margaret Thatcher's later call for wider share ownership and mass private home ownership financed by a mix of debt and the sale of public assets. Along with others, including leading figures in the Liberal and Labour parties, Meade favoured measures that would break up large concentrations of wealth and secure a much wider distribution of the ownership of private property, on the grounds that the benefits from capital ownership ought to be widely shared. Meade argued that this should be achieved, not by the state buying up private firms and then managing them, but by society establishing a growing stake in capital, either by investing budget surpluses (he was writing at a time when such surpluses were more common) in equities or by requiring firms to issue new shares annually to a public fund. It was the returns on the fund that could be used to pay a citizen's dividend.[9]

Although Meade's idea never got further than the drawing board, variants of it continued to surface. In 1971, a similar proposal was made by the Danish LO, the Confederation of Trade Unions and the Danish equivalent of the TUC, at its 1971 Congress, and then set out by the Danish Government in a Green Paper in 1971. The proposal – similar to the wage-earner funds adopted a decade later in Sweden – was for all employers to pay into a central workers' fund an amount related to the size of their wages bill, in annual increments of 0.5%, until a maximum of 5% was reached. Under the plan, each worker would receive an annual certificate setting out their entitlement in the fund, though these certificates could not be sold for at least seven years. To prevent them from being sold back for private ownership, they could not be sold in the open market, but only back to the fund itself. In the event, such a scheme was never implemented.

Also in the early 1970s, a similar proposal was examined in detail by a working group of the British Labour Party and published in an Opposition Green Paper – *Capital and Equality* – in 1973. The study group behind the Green Paper included the MPs Barbara Castle and Frank Judd along with the leading economists Sir Nicholas Kaldor and Lord Diamond, the latter appointed to chair Labour's Royal Commission on the Distribution of Income and Wealth in 1975. A related idea for a state investment fund (though funded by an estate tax paid in assets, so that society would participate in the capital gains from rising asset values) had also been considered, but rejected, by the Labour Party in the 1950s.[10]

The working party took as its starting point: 'in what ways could a Labour Government ensure that workers and the community share fully in the growth of company wealth, while at the same time, doing nothing to hamper the investment efforts of companies'.[11] Among the range of measures proposed was a 'capital sharing scheme' through a national Workers' Capital Fund in which all workers, private and public, would acquire over time equal wealth entitlements in the fund to be financed by the compulsory issue of new shares – of the order of 1% of the total equity in the company, by all companies over a given size. Also inherent to the scheme was the goal of 'extending opportunities for economic democracy, by giving Fund members – through their ownership of shares – direct powers over key financial decisions such as mergers, capital movements or investment in overseas subsidiaries'.[12] Again, the scheme was remarkably similar in broad outline to the Danish proposal and the Swedish scheme adopted in the early 1980s.

Meade's own ideas continued to be debated long after his original proposal. In the mid-1980s, he was a member of the SDP's Economic Policy Committee, and argued for a citizens' trust to be paid for by capital dilution, through the issue of new shares by firms, at a fraction of their existing share holdings, into the trust. An SDP working party estimated that, at a modest dilution rate of 1.5% (with firms issuing 1.5 new shares annually for every 100 existing shares), the state would build up a highly significant 50% share of the affected companies in about 50 years.[13]

Then in 1986, a resolution supporting the idea was put to the SDP's annual conference. Although it was strongly opposed by the leadership of the party as 'statist', the party's ruling body between conferences, the Council for Social Democracy, adopted it over the leadership's opposition.[14]

In 1989, Paddy Ashdown, leader of the new Liberal Democratic party, argued in a book, *Citizens' Britain*, for a 'Citizens' Share Ownership Trust', a development of Meade's ideas, aimed at giving everyone a direct stake in the economy. Ashdown argued that Thatcherism's claims to be creating a 'people's capitalism' rang hollow.

He urged the Liberal Democrats to 'be much more radical about popular share ownership – we could give every citizen a stake in our economy'.[15] To this end, he advocated a proposal drawn up by Meade for a 'Citizens' Share Ownership Unit Trust'. The ambition was for the fund to hold 10% of the assets of 'all private enterprises over a certain size'. This would make for 'a real, rather than make-believe, citizens' capitalism'.[16]

Shareholders: a privileged group

A scheme to socialise part of the ownership of companies would in some ways represent the mass extension of company-based employee ownership and profit-sharing schemes already operated by some companies, though with two key distinctions. A social wealth fund financed by the dilution of capital ownership would introduce the principle of profit sharing across *all* medium and large firms rather than just within particular firms. The benefits would be distributed collectively rather than to individual employees.

The concept of firm-based profit-sharing is already well embedded in the UK, especially among larger companies, and such schemes have been shown to have a number of benefits for individual firms. Of private sector UK companies with 10 or more employees, 8% offer their employees profit-sharing schemes, though this is below the European average of 14%.[17]

A social wealth fund financed in this way would not just lead to a more even spread of ownership, thus tackling one of the central drivers of inequality, but it would also help to deal with a number of problems with the current share ownership model and the chase for shareholder value.

Shareholders are a privileged group. They enjoy the immense advantage of limited liability, which limits their exposure to losses and other negative consequences of a company's actions. When things go wrong, it is taxpayers who pick up the bill, as they did in the aftermath of the 2008 crisis. Although corporation tax is in some senses a payment for this privilege, the size of this tax liability has been greatly eroded by both soaring levels of avoidance and by the global bidding down of corporate tax rates.[18]

As argued in Chapter Three, part of the gains from share ownership over time are unearned, a form of 'rentier' income. Just as Britain's overmighty financial sector is poor at creating (rather than extracting) wealth, the shareholder value model increasingly rewards capital owners through methods that are unrelated to the strengthening of the productive base:

- First, gains in share values over recent times have often been the result of corporate and financial manipulation rather than measurable improvements in corporate performance that bring wider economic benefits.[19] Much corporate activity, including the long corporate squeeze on wages and downsizing across British companies, driven by the chase for short-term 'shareholder value', has been geared to boosting share values and the enrichment of directors and, increasingly, absentee shareholders. As Andrew Haldane has argued persuasively, such shareholder short-termism has, by constraining investment, had long-term material costs for individual companies and the wider economy.[20]

- Second, the very concentration of ownership itself acts to inflate share (and other asset) values by creating excess demand for fixed assets. The rise of massive and increasingly mobile corporate and private cash surpluses that have followed from the diversion from wages to profits, and the growth in privately held wealth, have greatly fuelled the level of cash seeking a home. These pools of mobile money have not only acted to destabilise the global economy, and were a key contributing factor in the 2008 crash,[21] but they also serve to boost existing asset values, yielding windfall profits to owners and creating a reinforcing asset price spiral.

- Third, one of the important side-effects of the Bank of England's quantitative easing programme, through the purchase of financial assets, has been to further boost the wealth of those who own assets. As the Bank of England has shown, the policy is 'heavily skewed with the top 5% holding 40% of these assets'.[22] One evaluation has suggested that the programme has boosted the wealth of the top 5% by an average of £215,000.[23]

One of the benefits of a collective wealth fund financed by a levy on capital ownership would be to at least partially correct for these windfall gains, ensuring that at least a portion of them are captured for wider social use. Such an approach would also challenge the idea implicit to the dominant business model that the gains from the ownership of capital should be exclusive to owners.

So, how much revenue could be raised by such a levy? The total value of the shares held in the UK's top 100 companies amounts to £1.87 trillion (as at mid-September 2015). The value for all registered companies is higher at £2.26 trillion. A 0.5% and 1% annual levy just on the share ownership held in the top 100 companies would thus raise some £9 billion and £18 billion annually. More than half of these sums would be a charge on overseas owners.

Many practical issues remain with the idea of a social wealth fund paid for by capital dilution. What dilution or rate of levy on shareholders should be set? Although pension funds and insurance companies hold less than a tenth of UK equities today (Table 2.1) compared with more than half in 1990, there would still be a modest impact on pension and insurance funds.[24] How far could such a fund, with its growing stake in corporate ownership, be used for the extension of workforce democracy?

There is also the question of the potential for such a fund to play the kind of shareholder activist role adopted in Norway, a potential that applies equally to other equity-based funds. The fund could use its ownership stakes in companies to influence corporate policy on issues such as the living wage or the treatment of small suppliers. In the UK, for example, the shareholder activism movement has played a key role in the promotion of the living wage. The management of such a fund could press for change on a number of fronts by, for example, promoting debate on issues from employee rights to appropriate levels of executive compensation.

While the main experiment in an accumulating community-based social fund – the Swedish wage-earner fund – was brief, its closure came at a time when the post-war era of social democracy was already being challenged and the right had started to seize the political initiative with its successful call for handing more power to markets and allowing business a bigger share of the cake. The idea might command wider support in an era when the power of capital is being much more widely questioned.

Finally, there is the critical issue of how such a fund should be used? Its returns could be used simply to top up the public investment and social fund, thus contributing, through boosted investment schemes, to higher levels of wealth creation.

Another more radical possibility would be for the fund to be used to pay an annual citizen's dividend or grant along the lines proposed by James Meade. Although not financed through capital dilution, such a dividend scheme has, as shown in Chapter Four, operated in Alaska for three decades. If used in this way, the scheme would represent a significant new method of redistribution, in this case directly from shareowners – a mix of domestic individuals, institutions and foreign owners – to all citizens on an equal basis. Part of the windfall gains from share ownership would be passed on to society as a whole.

The Alaskan approach is only one possible model for providing a citizen's payment. Other ways are possible, involving different kinds of funding and different levels of ambition. These range from one-off payments to a regular citizen's income. The idea of a citizen's grant originated with Thomas Paine. In *Agrarian Justice*, published in 1795, he called for the creation in every nation of 'a national fund, to pay to every person, when arriving at the age of twenty-one years, the sum of fifteen pounds sterling, to enable him or her to begin the world! ... It is a right, and not a charity.'[25] This sum, he argued, should be paid for by a tax on personal wealth left at death.

In more recent times, the idea of an unconditional capital payment – an example of 'asset-based welfare' aimed at helping families to build assets and tackling one of the key elements of inequality – has been promoted by a number of writers and organisations. An idea for an inheritance-tax-funded 'citizen's inheritance' has been advocated by the political theorist Stuart White. He examines which is a fairer society: one in which nearly all personal wealth is passed on privately, with only light taxation, thus perpetuating historic wealth inequalities and the unequal opportunities that go with it; or one in which a larger portion of personal historic capital is shared in a way which guarantees everyone an inheritance and the social gains that that brings?[26]

Others have advocated the provision of 'baby bonds' aimed at evening out the significant differences in life chances that stem from wealth inequality.[27] The case for such bonds, given to each child at birth, has been stimulated in part by US evidence that the poor can build significant assets with the right jump-start.[28] This finding was supported by a UK study from the Institute of Education, which found that having even very modest savings at age 23 had a range of beneficial economic, social and health effects 10 years later.[29]

In 2002, the Labour government introduced just such a scheme – the Child Trust Fund – which provided a one-off lump sum to all children born after 1 September 2002. This was to be accessed at the age of 18, and could be topped up by friends and relatives. The scheme involved a universal and means-tested element. All families initially received a £250 voucher, while children from low-income households qualified for an extra £250. The amount actually received at 18 will depend on how much it is topped up by parents and the rate of return achieved on the invested sum. Although the scheme was successful in raising savings rates, it was abolished by the incoming coalition government in 2010 as part of the initial package of public spending cuts.[30] Those who benefited for the period it was operating will still receive their endowment when they reach 18.

A citizen's dividend or a capital grant is only one possible way forward. A much more ambitious approach would be to help fund a regular citizen's income, to be discussed in Chapter Seven

SEVEN

An income for all: can a citizen's income work?

There is now a growing debate in the UK, and elsewhere, about the merits of a citizen's income – a tax-free, unconditional and non-contributory basic weekly income paid to every individual as of right. A citizen's income, sometimes called a 'basic income', would transform the system of income support. It would pay every citizen an income, irrespective of how much they earned or their work status, administered in a similar way to Child Benefit, and which would replace much of the existing social security system.

The concept of a citizen's income has a long pedigree. It has been promoted over time by a great diversity of prominent British, American and European thinkers. Writing in 1795, Thomas Paine was one of its first proponents. A similar idea was backed by the British philosopher Bertrand Russell in 1919.[1] In 1950, Peter Drucker, the highly influential American management theorist, proposed a 'predictable income', which would 'banish the uncertainty, the dread of the unknown and the deep feelings of insecurity under which the worker today lives.'[2]

Since then, a long list of leading economists, politicians and campaigners, of diverse views, have called for such a scheme. They include JK Galbraith, Friedrich von Hayek, Martin Luther King Jr,

Paul Samuelson, James Tobin, Milton Friedman, Charles Murray, Tony Atkinson and, of course, James Meade (see Chapter Six).

Significantly, and unusually for such a radical change, a citizen's income has gained support across the political spectrum, from Right and Left, from pro-marketeers as well as social democratic interventionists, though for very different reasons. The Left has seen such a scheme as a way of securing a robust income floor and of tackling poverty, but also as a means of promoting equal citizenship and of encouraging a more equal distribution of income. For them, it is a recognition that all citizens have the right to some minimal claim on national income.

The Right, on the other hand, has favoured a citizen's income as a way of minimising state action in other areas, of offering both a safety net and continued freedom of choice. The highly influential pro-market theorist Friedrich von Hayek was a strong advocate: 'The assurance of a certain minimum income for everyone, or a sort of floor below which nobody need fall even when he is unable to provide for himself … is a legitimate protection against a risk common to all.' von Hayek did not see a citizen's income as a means of producing what he called a 'just distribution of income', merely as an efficient way of providing insurance, and perfectly consistent otherwise with free markets.[3]

Milton Friedman took a similar view. 'We should replace the ragbag of specific welfare programs with a single comprehensive program of income supplements in cash — a negative income tax,' he wrote in 1960 with his wife, Rose Friedman . 'It would provide an assured minimum to all persons in need, regardless of the reasons for their need, while doing as little harm as possible to their character, their independence, or their incentives to better their own conditions.'[4]

A negative income tax is an income tax system where people earning below a certain amount receive an income supplement to top it up. This cash credit is then withdrawn gradually as earnings rise. Although administered in a very different way, a negative income tax would have a similar outcome to a citizen's income.

The merits of a citizen's income

A citizen's income scheme has many merits. Aimed at guaranteeing a minimum, secure income for all – adults and children – whatever their circumstances, it would revolutionise the way income support is organised, while offering a number of improvements over the existing means-tested and overpunitive model of social security.

It would constitute a significant extension of the universal model of welfare, creating a safety net from which no-one would be excluded. Because such a scheme would aim to replace a number of existing means-tested benefits, it would relieve the problems of low take-up, the poverty trap and stigma associated with the current system. All of these have been exacerbated by the growth of means-testing over recent decades, notably through the growing role played by Housing Benefit, Working Tax Credit and Pension Credit.[5] For those of working age, around two-thirds of benefits were means-tested in 2010/11 compared to just over a quarter in 1980.[6] The government's universal credit scheme, to replace most of the existing benefits system, is in effect a giant means-tested scheme, further eroding the principle of universalism.

Under a citizen's income, means-testing would become more marginal, as originally intended by Beveridge. Because of this, additional earned income would not be reduced so sharply by the withdrawal of a range of means-tested benefits as in the existing system. Citizen's income would be cheap to administer and automate, saving large sums currently spent on processing claims, policing benefit claimants and assessing eligibility. Indeed, Department for Work and Pensions running costs stood at £8 billion in 2014/2015 and HM Revenue & Customs tax credit administration and write-offs at £2 billion.[7] Because of its greater simplicity, such a scheme would also greatly reduce the potential of fraud along with the number of assessment errors.

The principle of payments to citizens as of right already exists in the present system. Child Benefit is, in essence, a basic income for children, albeit at a modest rate, paid without a test of means. (Since

2013, additional tax is now charged on taxpayers earning over £50,000 living in households that receive Child Benefit – the High Income Child Benefit Tax Charge – aimed at clawing back Child Benefit from higher-income households.)

From 2016/17, the current basic state pension and the second pension will be combined into a single-tier scheme paying a flat-rate pension. This new flat-rate payment bears some comparison with how a CI would work, although because the payment – expected to be around £150 per week – will be below the poverty level, pensioners with low income will still be entitled to receive means-tested Pension Credit. To replace the existing system with an unconditional non-means-tested citizen's pension sufficient to do away with Pension Credit would require a higher flat-rate payment. It would also need to be extended to all pensioners, not just those who have paid sufficient national insurance contributions.[8]

It would overcome one of the principal flaws in the present system: its inability to ensure a guaranteed minimum income. Many people in need fall through the net because of the growing complexity of rules over entitlement and the growing influence of 'stick' over 'carrot'. The much tougher system of sanctions introduced by the coalition government in 2013 has led to close to one million recipients being denied benefits altogether, from a minimum of four weeks up to three years. In a large number of cases, this has resulted in individuals and families running out of money entirely, leading to severe hardship and sometimes destitution for those with no other source of income.

Advocates have also argued that an unconditional income would provide more freedom and choice. By providing basic security, a citizen's income would give people more time and more bargaining power in the labour market. With a growing debate about how to balance work–life commitments in a much more insecure work environment, a citizen's income would offer people greater flexibility between work and leisure, over education, and over the type and length of employment, while providing greater opportunity for wider caring and other community responsibilities. Some might choose to work less or take longer breaks between jobs. Others would be incentivised to start businesses. Some might drop out of work entirely, while others might devote more time to leisure, personal care or community support and less time to paid work.

'People would no longer feel forced to do menial or difficult jobs that they would otherwise undertake reluctantly or for reasons of survival,' writes Rajesh Makwana, the Director of Share the World's Resources. 'This would leave them free to devote more time to creative, cultural and caring pursuits, sparking a much-needed debate on the nature and purpose of work.'[9]

The opening up of greater choice would be especially beneficial to women. A universal citizen's income treats women as an individual unit, not as part of a household, giving them the potential of greater economic independence. Women disproportionately suffer from low wages, so a citizen's income could help to alleviate them from the poverty trap. Importantly, a citizen's income would both acknowledge and provide financial support for the mass of unpaid work, disproportionately undertaken by women, in childcare, care for the elderly and voluntary help in the wider community.

Another key advantage is that a citizen's income would provide a more robust system of support in today's much more fragile economic climate. It would be a very effective tool for tackling growing economic risk, and especially the rise of technological unemployment. Many advocates, including James Meade, have supported a citizen's income because of their fear that the process of technological change would greatly weaken the job prospects of large sections of the population.

Of course, this view of the impact of rapid technological advance may, as in previous periods of rapid change, turn out to be less bleak than these predictions. While the technological and digital revolution will create lots of disruption, it may also offer huge opportunities for job creation and productivity gains, albeit with unpredictable lags.

In 1931, in *The Economic Possibilities for Our Grandchildren*, JM Keynes predicted that by 2030, the growth of productivity would have created a society sufficiently rich that most people would choose more leisure and less work. The big social issue would be how to use abundant free time. In the event, Keynes was right about technological progress, but wrong about leisure. In the UK and the US, work has become more unequally distributed, with hours of work actually rising in recent times.

The new technological revolution opens up a possible route to the vision set out by Keynes. But that vision would only be realised if the inevitable disruption is minimised, the productivity gains are more equally shared and the losers compensated. If the winners end up enriching themselves irrespective of the wider fallout, then the inequality gap will widen sharply. The task for policy makers over the next decade and beyond will be to manage this process.

Through greater socialisation of national wealth, social wealth funds offer one possible way of providing greater protection.

A citizen's income is another tool that could help to realise the new potential for choice offered by new technology, and ensure that any losses are minimised. Indeed, these risks greatly reinforce the case for a citizen's income. Many of those writing about the growing distributional impact of accelerated automation and other drivers of change see the solution in a guaranteed income scheme. In Belgium, a citizen's income has been promoted by the philosopher Philippe Van Parijs as a way of promoting social justice given that 'equality of opportunity' cannot really be achieved.[10] In his 1995 book *The End of Work*, the American analyst Jeremy Rifkin concluded that the most effective way to at least partially protect those who would become displaced by machinery would be through a guaranteed income.[11] Martin Ford argues that the most effective solution to the disruptive impact of automation is 'some form of basic income guarantee'.[12] In the UK, the idea has also been strongly promoted by the academic Guy Standing, in his book on 'the precariat'[13] and by the UK-based Citizen's Income Trust.[14]

A further benefit of such a scheme is that it would have an important macroeconomic impact. One of the significant negative effects of the imbalance between wages and profits has been the long-term erosion of economic demand. This was a significant contributing factor to the 2008 financial crisis and the slowness of the recovery, and is now raising the risk of future instability. Technological advance is likely to intensify this problem, as the wage gains from automation are unlikely to match the gains to productivity, with capital grabbing a disproportionate share of the gains. As one writer in the *Los Angeles Times* has argued, echoing Walter Reuther:

> the relentless drive by capital to cut costs and boost profits is threatening to destroy the wellspring of economic growth that capitalism requires ... when there are no jobs for humans, there will be no consumers with the disposable income to buy the products being so efficiently produced by robots.[15]

A similar warning comes from the distinguished American economist and Nobel Laureate Robert Solow. Under new automated systems, he warns, 'the wage will absorb only a small fraction of all that output. The rest will be imputed to capital ... The ownership of capital will have to be democratized ... (through) some form of universal dividend.'[16] By helping to correct for this imbalance, a regular citizen's payment financed, in effect, by lowering the return to capital, would help to overcome this demand deficiency. It would also open up the option for policy makers, during recessions, of using quantitative easing to pay for a one-off higher payment rate, thus providing an immediate boost to consumer demand.

The critics

None of this means that a citizen's income has gained universal approval. Despite its many merits, there are a number of practical and philosophical issues with the introduction of such a scheme. Is it possible to set the payment at a level that provides enough for an acceptable standard of living? Or would a citizen's income only be able to meet a portion of basic living costs, as with Child Benefit at the moment? If the latter, some additional means-tested support would need to be retained, to top up the incomes of those who need it, thus retaining some of the complexities of the existing system.

If a citizen's income scheme were to be phased in over time, starting perhaps with an annual dividend or low weekly payment, how long a transition period would be needed? How would the transition process be managed to avoid the administrative problems of such a major change, such as those encountered in the early phase of Universal Credit? With such a scheme involving big changes in people's individual incomes, who would win and who would lose?

Because a flat-rate payment makes no allowance for those with additional needs, some suggest that there is an element of rough justice at work. Part of the reason that the present system is complex is that it attempts to deal with variations in personal circumstances, ones that an oversimplified system cannot deal with. To tackle this, a citizen's income either has to be very generous to deal with these extra needs (which pushes up the cost) or some types of means-testing need to stay, even if this means undermining the benefits of simplicity. Any citizen's income system would, for example, need to be supplemented with the continuation of disability benefits.[17]

Some argue that the public might resent an end to work conditionality, with all citizens being given equal support, irrespective of their contributions to society or work ethic, and that a universal system would mean money going unnecessarily to the richest in society. There is also the question of the impact on the incentive to work. Would a citizen's income help to create a 'money-for-nothing' culture, with some of the workforce either opting out of work or opting to work less? While critics argue that work would be discouraged, supporters claim that a citizen's income would, by greatly reducing the impact of the poverty trap, help to prevent the poorest sections of society from falling into benefit dependency and being discouraged from entering paid employment for fear of losing benefit entitlements.

The limited evidence from experiments with schemes suggests, in fact, that the number dropping out of the labour force is likely to be small. In the 1970s, there were four temporary trials with local Negative Income Tax schemes in the United States, and one in Canada called 'Mincome'. Analyses of the experiments found a modest decline in labour supply. There was a small level of dropout among primary earners (of the order of 5%) and higher among secondary earners (notably young mothers, teenagers in education and those about to retire) and some workers taking longer between jobs. The trials also showed that such systems help to relieve problems associated with means-testing, from incentives to take-up, while allowing greater freedom of choice over work–life issues.[18]

In addition, very limited citizen's income schemes have been piloted in Namibia and India.

- In 2007-09, Namibia, one of the poorest countries in the world, piloted a scheme in two villages. Initiated by the Basic Income Grant (BIG) group – a coalition of five large umbrella bodies including the Council of Churches, the project gave adults and children about US$12 a month (less than half the UN extreme poverty threshold of US$1 a day). The limited evidence from the experiment is that the payment did not discourage recipients from working, and the BIG coalition is continuing to press the Namibian government to introduce such a scheme as the best way of fighting poverty in the country.

- In India, there have been two pilot projects. One, funded by Unicef, introduced a basic income to adults in eight villages in Madhya Pradesh, paid directly into bank and cooperative accounts. The experiment involved a payment to 6,000 village participants, all of them poor. The payment started at 200 rupees per month (about US$3.75/€2.80) per adult and 100 rupees per child in initial pilots and was then raised to 300 rupees per month in later stages. This was estimated to be around 20–30% of the expected income of the households of participants and represented about 40% of the bare subsistence level.

- The other pilot, supported by the Delhi government, gave households a choice between continuing to receive food rations in an existing scheme or taking a monthly cash transfer instead. Many opted for the cash. Positive results were found in terms of nutrition, health, education, housing and infrastructure, and economic activity.

There was an improvement in access to medical treatment, while school attendance in the cash transfer villages rose sharply.[19]

- While some critics have claimed that a citizen's income would reduce labour supply, these experiments suggest a rise in income-earning work, even among these impoverished communities, with women gaining more than men. Economic activity rose in large part because the receipt of the citizen's income reduced the risk for participants starting their own enterprises.[20]

Of course, the impact of a pilot scheme in poor countries may be a limited guide to what would happen in richer countries.

Significantly, a citizen's income scheme would involve a shift from the Beveridge principle of national insurance based on the sharing of risk to a system of guaranteed income as of right. As the New Economics Foundation has argued, a citizen's income is 'an individualised measure, not a collective one, focusing resources on providing everyone with an income at all times rather than on pooled risk-sharing mechanisms which provide help for everyone when they need it.'[21]

While the national insurance principle has served Britain well for more than half a century and has always been popular with public opinion, it has been steadily eroded. In many ways, the Beveridge system of social insurance – which was initiated in 1948 for an era of full employment and with most people in long-term work – has failed to keep pace with wider economic changes, and especially the ongoing upheaval in labour markets and the rise of flexible working patterns. It is much less suited to an era when the majority of the workforce move in and out of the labour force and between jobs throughout their lives.

The cost of the social security system also greatly outweighs contributions. Over time, there has been a substantial shift away from the founding post-war principle of a universal, contributory system, in which benefits were treated as an entitlement, with receipt dependent on circumstances (bringing up children, being unemployed, disabled or elderly), not on an assessment of financial need. In part because of these failings, the current social security system enjoys a declining level of public trust.

Certainly, solutions would need to be found to some of these wider questions, while a citizen's income would only provide a partial solution to the issue of growing poverty and deepening inequality. The debate around citizen's income also has to address the arguments of pro-market advocates. These support it in part because it encourages greater individual freedom and less state intrusion, and would see its introduction as an opportunity to sweep away a range of other types of social protection.

Yet a citizen's income scheme would not replace other welfare support measures but would complement them. 'Although, in my opinion, it would bring huge benefits, an unconditional citizen's income is not a magic solution to all political, social and economic problems,' according to the labour market specialist Ursula Huws. 'I believe that it could be one ingredient in the development of a kind of welfare state that is deserving of the name. However it is only one ingredient among several.'[22]

There is, for example, a tangible risk that employers might take advantage of such a scheme to cut pay, shifting labour costs from companies to society as a whole. The setting of a decent and properly enforced national minimum wage rate would therefore continue to be necessary, to minimise this risk. To work, such a scheme would need to be reinforced by other measures, not just a strong minimum wage, but also high-quality public services and reforms that made the tax system more progressive. A minimalist scheme, of the sort favoured by right-of-centre advocates, and used to justify the cutting back of other aspects of welfare support and state intervention, would be a dangerous animal indeed.

Can the cost be met?

The central issue with a generous citizen's income is that the *gross* cost would be high, much higher than the existing social security budget. This is because it involves a payment going to every citizen.

The higher the payment, the higher the gross cost. Against this, there would be substantial offsetting savings, as the payments would aim to replace some existing means-tested and contributory benefits (as well as existing personal tax allowances), and there would be significant administrative savings.

In an ideal scheme, the state benefits that would be withdrawn include Jobseeker's Allowance, Working Tax Credit and the state pension.[23] Some means-tested benefits would remain, including Council Tax support and Housing Benefit, in order to prevent considerable losses, including for the growing numbers facing high housing rents. There has been a sharp rise in the cost of means-tested Housing Benefit to compensate for the move over time to market and near-market rents in private and social housing. Without a way of lowering housing costs, the current system of means-tested Housing Benefit would have to remain.

There have now been several attempts to simulate the impact of a scheme using a mix of different payment levels, configurations of the tax system and withdrawal of existing means-tested benefits. Each leads to a different pattern of winners and losers and different overall net costs.

A study by Malcolm Torry, Director of the Citizen's Income Trust, tested a scheme that replaced most means-tested benefits (excluding only Housing Benefit, Council Tax support and Pension Credit) and paid weekly benefits of £145 to pensioners, £71.70 to other adults and £56.80 per child. In order to ensure revenue neutrality, at zero net cost, the scheme required an increase in the basic rate of income tax to 25p in the pound, the introduction of a higher rate of 50p in the pound, an increase in national insurance rate above the current threshold from 2p to 12p in the pound and the reduction of the lower earnings limit to zero. This has the effect of making national insurance contributions payable on all earned income at 12%. Moreover, while the scheme would have been revenue-neutral, it would have left 28% of households in the lowest decile worse off by more than 10%.[24] This, as the study acknowledged, is much too high a level of loss and a feasible scheme would require finding a solution to the 'loser problem'.

One lesson from these and other simulations is that it is very difficult to design a revenue-neutral scheme that pays a decent sum and withdraws most means-tested benefits without significant numbers of losers, even with increased tax rates. This is because the current benefits system, partly because of its complexity and reliance on means-testing, is able to pay large sums to some groups. A simpler, flat-rate citizen's income scheme cannot compensate for the withdrawal of both personal tax allowance and most means-tested benefits without becoming expensive.

Another important implication is that, in some configurations, the main gainers from a citizen's income are likely to be those with modest earnings rather than the poorest households.[25] This is because any additional withdrawals in taxation from their income are likely to be lower than the loss of benefits in the present system. As noted by Donald Hirsch, Director of the Centre for Research in Social Policy at Loughborough University, such a move would, as a result, improve the incentive to work and possibly raise public support for such a scheme.[26]

These findings do not mean that a citizen's income scheme is infeasible. There are several ways of tackling these problems. One option, explored by Torry and others, would be for a partial CI scheme that paid a lower rate, but that left in place the means-tested benefits system and reduced households' means-tested benefits by taking into account their CIs when benefits were calculated. Such a scheme could be revenue-neutral, could reduce losses among the poorest to almost zero and could be implemented almost overnight.[27] It could also be seen as a first step in a process towards a more generous scheme.

Such a 'partial' scheme would still require a modest increase in the basic rate of tax, would be broadly redistributive from rich to poor and, significantly, would reduce the number of children in poverty by as much as 40%. There would be fewer households on means-tested benefits, and those still on them would receive less help in this way. This would make them less dependent on means-testing than under the present system. Such a scheme would be a hybrid. Although it would fall short of an ideal scheme and retain some of the complexity of the existing system, it would contain a genuine unconditional income and would deliver many of the benefits of such a scheme.[28] It would have an additional and important strength. By reducing the role of means-testing and guaranteeing an income for all, albeit it a modest rate, it would greatly rebalance the existing system of social security in favour of universalism. Such a scheme could be implemented in the UK. It would reduce poverty substantially, for a modest increase in the basic rate of income tax, and, for the first time, introduce a guaranteed income floor.

A second option would be to introduce a citizen's income scheme in stages, for example by starting with children through a substantial boost in the level of Child Benefit. A £56.80 child payment would be revenue-neutral, but would require an increase in the standard rate of tax to 24.5% and a four percentage point increase in national insurance payments above the threshold. Although there would be some losers, these would all be among higher income groups.[29]

There is a strong case for raising the level of Child Benefit substantially as a particularly effective way of reducing poverty and inequality, as well as being a first step in the introduction of a citizen's income. Tony Atkinson, for example, has argued the case for 'a universal basic income for children' that should be introduced across the European Union.[30] Instead, the value of Child Benefit has been falling, set to lose a quarter of its real value between 2010 and 2020.

A third option would be to introduce a fully fledged scheme but with substantial additional funding. Even a more modest scheme paying lower rates would require some increase in the standard rate of income tax. Because of the difficulties with making a full, revenue-neutral scheme work, a scheme that minimised the number of losers without a politically sensitive hike in tax rates would probably need an injection of around £20 billion annually. This is where a joint social wealth fund/citizen's income scheme as advocated by Meade and others could come in.

This extra funding does not need to come from an additional increase in existing or traditional taxation. It could come from the revenue from a targeted citizen's income social wealth fund specifically aimed at providing the additional funding through new charges on capital and wealth, some of them paid in the form of shares. One possibility for paying for such a fund would be through a new shareholder levy, discussed in Chapter Six. Of course, the revenue from a new levy on capital – and new taxes on unearned gains or economic rent from common wealth – can only be used once and there are clear trade-offs in how such revenue might be used. If new charges on capital, for example, were used to part-fund a citizen's income scheme, they could not also be used to fund a public investment and social fund.

EIGHT

From the drawing board to reality

There is a powerful case for introducing one or more social wealth funds and a citizen's income scheme in the UK, but just how politically feasible are these ideas? Could one or more social wealth funds be introduced in the UK, funded in the ways suggested earlier?

- Could they be linked to the introduction of a citizen's payment or income scheme?
- Can such schemes jump from the drawing board to reality, or are they little more than the utopian mutterings of a few fringe academics, policy wonks and campaigners?

Social wealth funds

The principles underlying social wealth funds are being more widely debated and accepted, while pressure for their establishment has been growing from think tanks, pressure groups and a growing number of commentators. Significantly, such support extends across the political spectrum, perhaps a necessary condition for their realisation.

In 2013, the independent Intergenerational Foundation launched a report arguing that the creation of social wealth funds 'would be a tangible way for government to show they care about future generations by the way they manage their revenue and resources.'[1] The principle of such funds has been discussed in publications by the influential think tanks the Institute for Public Policy Research (IPPR) and the Royal Society of Arts.[2]

A report by the IPPR has proposed hypothecating revenue from the UK's financial sector to pay for what they call a 'British Future Fund' to help meet future public expenditure requirements: 'This sovereign wealth-style fund would help support future public expenditure by "skimming" off the proceeds of large-scale private financial accumulation for public benefit'. The report, by Matthew Lawrence, argues that such a fund would operate as a profit-making body, managed independently of ministerial direction, under clear ethical investment guidelines, and aim to accumulate over time a portfolio of assets within the financial sector. Part of the gains would be reinvested in growing the fund and part used to finance social investment. Over time, the fund would come to own a portfolio of assets within the financial sector, but without seeking to interfere in the day-to-day management of private firms. 'Essentially it would act as a silent "rentier" in terms of taking a capital share in the proceeds of financialisation and reaping the dividends.'[3]

Support for the principle of social wealth funds has also spread to leading political figures and advisers. In 2014, writing in the *Daily Telegraph*, the London mayor, Boris Johnson, advocated a 'citizens' wealth fund to be created to build the homes the country needs and finance the roads, railways and power stations'. Johnson advocated creating such a fund, not by any of the ways outlined above, but by pooling some of the UK's 39,000 disparate public pension funds into much larger funds, large enough to pay for a boost to infrastructure investment.[4]

The case for merging pension funds is widely recognised, and the government has been pressing, though mostly by nudge, for closer collaboration between funds in order to realise the benefits of increased scale. Michael Johnson, research fellow at the right-of-centre think tank the Centre for Policy Studies, has called for the Local Government Pension Scheme (LGPS) to be turned into a single investment vehicle:

'It is probably the most realistic route. The LGPS has £210-£220 billion in assets littered across 101 predominantly sub-scale, inefficient funds. It ought to be one fund.'[5]

British pension funds are smaller, more fragmented and lack the scale of funds compared with other countries, including the Netherlands' ABP US$375 billion) and Australia's Future Fund (US$92 billion). These larger funds are able to directly acquire stakes in large companies and invest in major infrastructure projects. Amalgamating the 101 local authority funds operating in Britain would bring together assets of over £200 billion, making it larger than most existing sovereign wealth funds.

In August 2015, Boris Johnson appointed Eddie Truell, chairman of the London Pensions Fund Authority (LPFA), and a strong advocate of pension scheme infrastructure investment, to encourage consolidation. Truell is a veteran City financier, who made his fortune as founder of Duke Street, the private equity firm, in 1998. 'Everyone is excited by the idea of creating a UK sovereign wealth fund that can invest in infrastructure to benefit UK [companies] and make a return for pensioners,' said Truell. 'The goal of the new wealth fund,' he added, 'is to save costs, pool resources, improve returns and provide funding for construction of UK infrastructure.'[6]

This amalgamation process is already underway. In December 2014, the London fund agreed a separate £10 billion partnership with the Lancashire County Pension Fund. Then in 2015, two UK public pension funds – the Greater Manchester Pension Fund (GMPF) and the LPFA – announced plans to form a joint infrastructure investment venture aimed at investing £500 million over three or four years. The GMPF is one of the largest public pension funds in the UK, with assets worth some £16 billion. Portions of the money are expected to be invested in transport, housing, urban regeneration and energy renewables projects, though the joint partnership has not yet committed to anything.

In the past, the LPFA has invested in Pontoon Dock in London's Docklands, while GMPF has long invested in its local area, including in a city centre office block in Manchester and local new housing schemes.[7] Nevertheless, to date, even large public pension funds have shied away from long-term infrastructural investment, in part because of the longer trajectories of return and regulatory restrictions. At the end of 2014, for example, the LPFA only had 3.5%, or £170 million, in such investment.

Much more could – and should – be done to use the financial power of pension funds to encourage a higher level of wealth creation. This would require much more direct action from government than the nudge approach adopted to date. Craig Berry, Deputy Director of the Sheffield Political Economy Research Unit, has called for the establishment of national and local economic renewal funds to be funded by near-compulsory allocations by all workplace pension schemes: 'Any individual or firm would be able to bid to the fund for investment, into projects consistent with improving the productive capacity of the UK economy. A more moderate version of this proposal would see existing pension schemes compelled to develop investment strategies more commensurate with the geographical location of their UK workforce.'[8]

Of course, pension funds are not community-owned assets. They do not belong to the government, nor do they belong to all the citizens of the UK; they are the property of the beneficiaries, and exist to serve their retirement needs. Although there is a strong case for pension funds to merge to increase efficiency and reduce management costs, and to invest more in long-term investment, such funds are different from social wealth funds and should be viewed as additional to, and not part of, such funds. Nevertheless, while the growing pressure to create larger pension funds able to fund urban investment will continue to mount, the debate has helped to add fire to the wider issue of the merits of social wealth funds and their underlying principles.

Ultimately, the creation of a British fund, or system of funds, will depend on getting a political consensus and much greater public awareness and support. Both are a necessary condition for their implementation. This echoes the experience elsewhere. In the US, local schemes operating in a number of states from Alaska to Wyoming enjoy support from both Republicans and Democrats and enjoy high levels of public support.

Some cross-party support for the principle of a UK fund already exists. Recent years have seen something of a political momentum to join the sovereign wealth fund club. The Scottish government has talked of creating a sovereign wealth fund for Scotland based on oil and gas revenues, though this was before the sharp fall in the oil price and the 2014 referendum vote.[9] A group of Labour MPs has suggested using the Crown estate, which manages the £8.6bn of land and property owned by the crown, to set up a UK social wealth fund to help finance public investment. In 2012, the estate generated a surplus of £253 million, representing an impressive 12% return. The MPs propose that the Crown estate should be given the freedom to invest in property markets, in promising businesses and in UK infrastructure.[10]

Significantly, the debate around the possible development of shale gas has given additional impetus to the idea of social wealth funds. This is a highly controversial area, and the future development of shale gas remains uncertain. Opponents have warned that exploiting the UK's shale gas reserves could push up greenhouse gas emissions, pollute local water resources, and divert investment from clean energy. Nevertheless, the debate around shale has generated new political commitments for the principle of collectivised funds.

In November 2014, the House of Lords debated an amendment to the Infrastructure Bill from the Conservative peer Lord Hodgson of Astley Abbotts. As Lord Hodgson wrote in the *Daily Telegraph*: 'My amendment provides an enabling framework for the establishment of a UK shale fund. It proposes, among other things, that no less than 50 per cent of government revenues from shale gas development should be put into [a sovereign wealth] fund; that no more than 4 per cent of the fund should be distributed each year – to ensure longevity; that those proceeds be devoted to long-term prospects; and finally, and most importantly, that there is a proper degree of governance and transparency in the management of the fund.'[11]

Lord Hodgson was acknowledging not just the clear principle of social wealth funds, but their need to be independent and fully transparent, operating openly and not behind closed doors. It was also a rebuke to government and the Treasury, which have always been wary of surrendering absolute day-to-day control over any aspect of the country's financial affairs.

Echoing the arguments for sharing the gains from natural resources, for both current and future generations, Lord Hodgson continued, 'More importantly, it is about inter-generational fairness and equity. These gas reserves have been built up over millions of years. Are they properly ours to plunder and spend in a few generations? Should we not ensure that some part of their proceeds is left for our successors?' In an online poll linked to the article, the *Daily Telegraph* asked: 'Should money made from shale gas be saved for a rainy day in a sovereign wealth fund?' In an admittedly small and self-selecting response, 93% said yes, 7% said no.

Leading ministers are also now taking the principle of social wealth funds seriously. The chancellor, George Osborne, has suggested that a shale gas fund could be created and targeted at the north of England where, if it happens, much of the UK's fracking activity would be expected to take place. 'You could create a sovereign wealth fund for the money that comes from the shale gas that we're going to be pulling out of the ground, particularly in the north of England,' Osborne told BBC Radio 4's *Today* programme in 2014. 'That's a way of making sure this money is not squandered on day-to-day spending but invested in the long-term economic health of the north.'[12]

Before the 2015 election, the influential Conservative Home website called for 'the creation of a UK Sovereign Wealth Fund into which all new public windfall revenues – for instance, the tax revenues from offshore gas and oil extraction – would be paid'. A similar, if weaker and narrower promise made it into the Conservative Party's election manifesto: 'the shale gas resources of the North [will be] used to invest in the future of the North'.[13] A similar pledge to 'invest any tax profits from "fracking" into setting up a Sovereign Wealth Fund to pay for elderly care' also appeared in UKIP's 2015 election manifesto.

In July 2015, the *Financial Times* reported that a 'new wave of support has emerged for the creation of a UK sovereign wealth fund, which proponents believe would pump much-needed money into large infrastructure projects.'[14] Senior figures in the fund management industry – which of course stands to benefit significantly from being commissioned to help with their management – have also been warming to the idea.

Rob Thomas, director of research at a financial consultancy and a former Bank of England economist, has called for the proceeds of quantitative easing to be used to establish a sovereign wealth fund. 'Rather than buying gilts, you could take the same money and put it into real physical investments,' he wrote. 'You get a better return and it makes the economy stronger for the long term.'[15]

Newton Investment Management hosted a conference in 2015 in partnership with Cambridge University on the potential for a British sovereign wealth fund. 'One obvious negative [of the current high levels of debt] is the impact on growth,' says Helena Morrissey, chief executive of Newton Investment Management, 'and the creation of a sovereign wealth fund could go some way to correcting this.'[16]

Asked whether a UK sovereign wealth fund would be a sensible idea, Euan Munro, chief executive of Aviva Investors, the fund management arm of the FTSE 100-listed insurer, said: 'Yes. It would go some way to correcting how short-term thinking is leading to under-investment in critical infrastructure. Done well, this will increase the long-term productive capacity of the economy, and would benefit everyone.'[17]

The case for social wealth funds is now firmly established and has been gathering support across influential opinion. Such funds would represent a new and innovative economic instrument. Depending on how they are funded, they have the potential to address a number of the big political issues facing the UK from the growing concentration of economic capital to the inadequate level of public and private investment.

They have been used with telling effect in other countries and there are a number of overseas schemes that could be drawn on to create a British version. Providing that such schemes – launched at a local as well as a national level – are operated in a transparent and open way, and are seen to benefit the community more widely, they also have the potential to be highly popular.

There is now no overriding economic or political reason why Britain should not proceed to create its own social wealth fund, or portfolio of funds. And, given that such funds will take time to grow and take effect, the less delay the better. There are a number of potential sources of finance, some of which, including a levy on some commercial activity such as on successful mergers and acquisitions, would be more contentious than others.

Perhaps the most controversial of these sources would be the application of a levy on shareholders used to pay a citizen's dividend on the Alaskan model, or more ambitiously, a citizen's income. Such a twin-based scheme would involve a transfer from shareholders to citizens and has the potential to redress the excessive concentration of wealth and to dilute the overdominance of capital in the economy.

A citizen's income

Although the idea of a citizen's income has begun to be more widely debated, and there is a growing body of opinion supporting the idea, that support is not as well advanced politically as that for social wealth funds and has yet to penetrate mainstream political thinking.

A citizen's income scheme would challenge traditional approaches to economic and social policy. It would deal with a number of weaknesses with the existing social security model, which has become, in many ways, a much weaker tool for social protection, and would provide a much firmer base of income security in an increasingly fragile economic and social environment.

The post-war social security system was born in very specific circumstances and was designed to fit a particular sort of economy as a system of contributory insurance against a range of economic risks. The Beveridge system worked well in the post-war era, when those risks were better controlled. The goal of full employment was largely met, jobs were much more secure (often for life), wages were more generous relative to contemporary needs than has been true in more recent years, and housing costs were much lower as a ratio of net income.

Today the risk of unemployment is higher, low pay and work insecurity have spread and relative housing costs have risen sharply. These trends have greatly raised the risk of poverty and the demands on the social security and wider welfare system. Partly in consequence, the present system has become increasingly complex and poorly understood. It is unpopular with the public, though this is in part down to deliberate government misrepresentation. It has also become increasingly vulnerable politically, with the degree of social protection being greatly weakened for those of working age.

A citizen's income scheme would tackle some of these problems. By guaranteeing an income floor for all, it would help to compensate for the fragility of the modern labour market. It would also help to lessen the potential threat to livelihoods from accelerated automation, a trend that makes the case for citizen's income more compelling.

There have been several experiments with payments to citizens, though with differing reasons and history. The Alaskan scheme has been in place for a quarter of a century, but pays an annual dividend, not a weekly income. Britain initiated a Child Trust Fund, albeit briefly. The pilot schemes in Namibia and India were instructive, but have not been turned into anything more permanent.

In 2010, Iran became the first country in the world to establish a nationwide citizen's income. Interestingly, the scheme did not emerge by design but by default: 'it was the by-product of an effort to reform an outdated system of price subsidies that concerned primarily fuel products.'[18] The scheme was designed to compensate the population for the withdrawal of fuel price subsidies that had been costing US$100–120 billion a year. In essence, price subsidies have been converted into cash subsidies, with a cash payment of some $33 a month – short of a subsistence income – to most of the population. This is financed, as in Alaska, from oil revenues. The objective is twofold: improving economic efficiency by reducing fuel consumption; and reducing income disparities through cash transfers. Although almost the entire population of 75 million is now covered, a small proportion has decided not to claim it.

The introduction of the citizen's income in Iran was motivated not by a sense of right or entitlement, but to facilitate subsidy reform by making it more palatable to the public. In a sense, Iran stumbled upon basic income, while pursuing a different objective. Nevertheless, as one analyst of the scheme concluded, this 'unique experience highlights the instrumental potential of basic income in smoothing the way towards better resource allocation and greater equality, the two objectives of Iran's reform.'[19]

Alongside these examples, social groups have been pressing the case for a citizen's income in many developed nations. Germany has a strong supportive movement, with dozens of active groups and a good deal of media attention. There are active groups promoting the idea in the United States, Canada, Australia, New Zealand, Japan and the UK. In the US, the Basic Income Guarantee Network organises a national congress each year. In Spain a strong grassroots movement has been actively campaigning for the introduction of a basic income by means of a national popular legislative initiative. The campaign managed to obtain, by early 2015, approximately 185,000 signatures in support, though this was less than the threshold of 500,000 signatures required for the initiative to be examined by the national parliament.

Elsewhere, the idea has risen further up the political and public agenda. In Switzerland, a national referendum is to be held in 2016 on the implementation of a scheme. This has been triggered by the growth of popular support, with well over 100,000 signatures gathered in 2013, well above that needed to trigger a national referendum.[20] Switzerland is one of the few countries in the world that operates a system of direct democracy in which the Swiss people can ensure a national referendum on any topic, provided they gather enough signatures calling for a vote. The government then determines the timetable and the result is binding.

Two European nations have gone further still. The Finnish coalition government is seriously considering a pilot project for a basic income, generating widespread interest in how it might work. Such a move is supported by the Prime Minister, Juha Sipilä, and by a majority of MPs, though some ministers are opposed. There are also differences of view on what the concept means, with some supporting a scheme that is conditional and means-tested. With unemployment an increasing concern, and a live debate about the need for reforms to the country's complex and costly benefits system, seven out of ten Finns have said that they are in favour of a basic income, while the influential think tank, Sitra, has published a report which provides a roadmap for setting up a pilot project.[21]

The government is now looking at a limited, geographical experiment, probably in 2016, and has commissioned a report on how it might work. If it goes ahead, the likelihood is that under the pilot, participants from low-income groups and different locations would be paid four different monthly amounts, perhaps from €400 to €700. Though the details are yet to be confirmed, the experiment would aim to test the wider impact, including on employment and on the motivation to work.[22]

There is also growing interest in such a scheme in the Netherlands, prompted in part by the broadcast of two Dutch documentaries about basic income which have raised public awareness of the idea.[23] The City of Utrecht, the fourth most populated city, is planning a pilot project, probably in early 2016, while a number of other municipalities are also considering running similar pilots, among them the cities of Tilburg, Wageningen and Groningen. Such initiatives have come from within the municipal administrations, with encouragement from academics, local pressure and from the Dutch basic income network.[24] 'What is most interesting and a very good sign is that the initiatives come from people with all kinds of political backgrounds, and are often depoliticized,' is how the Dutch economist , Sjir Hoeijmakers, has described the Utrecht and other city initiatives.[25]

The Utrecht experiment is planned to work with six groups. One group will get something close to a basic income (no withdrawal if there is extra earned income and no further conditions), while a sixth group will stay living under the current welfare system and act as a control group. Each group will have a minimum of 50 people.

The developments in Finland and the Netherlands are also causing ripples elsewhere. In France, the southern region of Aquitaine is now considering a similar experiment to assess the viability of basic income. In July 2015, the regional council based in Bordeaux voted through a motion calling for such a pilot. The motion was supported by the Greens on the council, but also with enthusiasm by the radical left coalition and by one right-wing member, also deputy mayor of the city.[26]

The debate in the UK

In the UK, the debate about such a scheme is still at an early stage. Along with the Citizen's Income Trust, several organisations have launched investigations into the potential of such a scheme, including the Joseph Rowntree Foundation, the independent think tank, the Royal Society of Arts (RSA) and the pressure group Compass. Matthew Taylor, the head of the RSA has backed the idea of: 'A universal citizen's income: respecting human dignity and care, reducing state intrusion, incentivising work and boosting productivity.'[27] In 2015, the right-of-centre think tank the Adam Smith Institute called for the introduction of a negative income tax to replace tax credits, Jobseeker's Allowance and other means-tested benefits.[28]

Although some Liberal Democrats have called for a universal basic income to become party policy, the only political party to back a citizen's income is the Green Party.[29] In 2015, the Greens were advocating a scheme with a weekly adult payment of £72 a week.[30] The new shadow chancellor, John McDonnell, has expressed interest in the concept in the past.[31]

Nevertheless, while the idea of a citizen's income has been gathering wider support, a British version has a long way to go before it enters the public and political arena as a serious proposition. For that to happen, the debate on its merits – and downsides – needs to extended from campaigners and researchers into the public domain.

Some sense of the potential controversy surrounding such an idea came during the 2015 general election campaign. Because of the potential 'loser' problem, the Green's proposal became the subject of press scrutiny and controversy, forcing the party to drop the idea from its manifesto, while remaining committed to the idea as a long-term aspiration.

Of course, there are many hurdles that would need to be overcome before a citizen's income could become politically feasible, while its introduction would involve a transformation in:

- the pattern of social protection;
- the extent and pattern of redistribution;
- the nature of the tax system;
- the pattern of work incentives;
- current social and cultural attitudes;
- the existing political mindset.

As Donald Hirsch has commented, a citizen's income system would require 'seismic shifts in [public] attitudes and policy' before it would become acceptable. Would the public accept that 'everyone should be supported at a certain level, with no work-based condition' and 'that the basic marginal tax rate should be substantially higher than it is now'?[32] Certainly no scheme could be introduced until the public has debated the trade-offs involved and could be persuaded of its benefits. But while we are a long way from that, the idea of a citizen's income could be said to be at a similar stage in the debate surrounding a national minimum wage some years before it was finally implemented in 1999.

Despite the undoubted hurdles, the kind of partial scheme outlined earlier is economically feasible. It is certainly time for a much more serious and wide-ranging debate about the future of social protection. The present system is ill-equipped to deal with an increasingly fragile jobs market. It has become a safety net that is riddled with holes. Although a citizen's income would raise issues of its own, it would tackle many of the problems with the existing system. Such are its strengths, its time is surely coming.

NINE

Towards a sharing economy

The UK is an unacceptably divided society. The concentration of economic capital gives its owners a growing grip on the levers of both economic and political power. Inequality may be at the centre of the global political debate, but reducing the gap requires a strategy that raises the floor and lowers the ceiling and ensures a fairer spread of economic opportunities and social outcomes. It's an ambitious goal, and meeting it depends, critically, on measures that break up the great concentration of capital ownership.

Social wealth funds and a citizen's payment could both play a key part in a policy package aimed at creating a fairer society. The schemes would have different but supportive roles. Socialised funds could tap existing resources from a range of areas in a way which maintains a higher level of social capital, while a citizen's income scheme could provide a guaranteed level of social protection in today's more turbulent times.

Progressive social wealth funds are a potentially powerful new economic and social instrument. Some models are more radical than others. Those which socialised some elements of private capital have the potential to transform, over time, the pattern of inequality and opportunity.

A public ownership fund would provide a new national commitment that public assets should be held in common. Such a fund would help to limit the extent of private ownership and gain. The fund would protect existing assets, bringing an end to their arbitrary and politically driven sale aimed at buying short-term gain in the public finances. Instead, such assets would be preserved for the common good, protected for current and future generations. Such a fund could quickly mobilise assets that already exist and, allowed to grow over time, would provide a strong counterweight to the power of private capital.

A public investment and social fund would help to boost investment, thus contributing to productivity growth and eventually a higher wage floor and greater economic opportunity. It would also help to boost the UK's Britain's increasingly weakened social capital, targeted to improve opportunities among poorer communities. A social housing fund would increase the volume of social and affordable housing. A social care fund – paid for by a new social care tax on private housing wealth – would contribute extra funding, help to improve the quality of social care and ensure a more equitable distribution of payment.

Each of the funds would contribute in different ways to creating greater equality and improved life chances. The financing of social wealth funds would come from the better management of public assets along with the reallocation of some existing tax revenue and the introduction of enhanced or new taxation elsewhere, including on property wealth. Such an approach would also change the pattern and use of the public finances.

Such measures could not be implemented without public backing. Nevertheless, it is likely that the principles underpinning the funds, borrowed from best practice in other countries, would prove popular. A public ownership fund, effectively a giant pool of wealth owned in common, is also likely to gain public support as a new way of preserving and managing public assets, to help pay for new hospitals and schools and improved open spaces and social amenities. Its books would be open for scrutiny, with every citizen made aware of their share in such commonly held assets, thus emphasising their own stake in the economy. With the growing public unease about the declining access to decent housing and the political failure to tackle it, a social housing fund would be likely to prove a political winner. A social care fund paid for by new taxation on property wealth would undoubtedly prove controversial, but the funding of social care is a pressing issue that cannot be ducked indefinitely by political leaders.

Such funds would offer public clarity, reducing some of the complexity and confusion surrounding large parts of current social policy, while the national accounts in these areas would also be easier to digest. The funds could each be managed by a broadly based independent board, thereby ensuring a high degree of transparency and clear political independence, as in the case of the Norwegian Sovereign Wealth Fund. There is also no reason why the management of such funds should not be open to more direct public involvement, for example through the election of one or more citizens' representatives to the board. Such funds could be operated not just nationally, but at a regional and local level as well, and would help to restore some of the current imbalance between capital, citizen and the state.

These measures would contribute to a more balanced model of capitalism. There would be a stronger state role in investment and in managing the public finances for the wider good. There would be a limit to the process of privatisation. While some models would have only a modest impact on the overall pattern of capital ownership, other more radical schemes would have a much bigger impact on the degree of socialisation over time.

A citizen's payment and/or income could also play a key role in the development of a more progressive model of political economy. A citizen's income would help to address, directly, the growing crisis of work insecurity and low wages and the mounting problems with a heavily means-tested and unpopular social security system. The idea is not yet as well advanced as that of social wealth funds, but is being more widely debated within the UK. Because of its potential to provide a more secure system of income support in a more fragile economic and social era, it is likely to rise up the political agenda. With different versions of such schemes close to being piloted in some European nations, it may not be long before pressure mounts to implement a pilot in the UK.

Both social wealth funds and a citizen's income are independent ideas that do not have to be implemented together. Nevertheless, a dual scheme with a citizen's income part-funded from a targeted levy-based social wealth fund may be the key to its viability.

Neither proposal offers short-term solutions. As with the best overseas examples, both would take time to build. Nevertheless, there are no economic or political reasons why the UK should not now launch one or more social wealth funds. A public ownership fund, for example, could become fully operational within the course of a single parliament, though it might take longer to deliver significant returns. Because of inevitable transition issues, a citizen's income scheme might take longer to implement, though the kind of more modest scheme outlined in Chapter 7 could be introduced more quickly, possibly as a first step in the transition to a more ambitious model.

As both would take time to develop, and are essentially long term in nature, such schemes would need cross-political support before they could be launched. Although there might be opposition from segments of the corporate and financial establishment, such changes would eventually lead to a stronger economic and social base, as they have done elsewhere. Some parts of the financial services industry would be harnessed to play a role in managing funds and helping to leverage the resources available.

In recent years, policy change has greatly lagged behind wider economic and social developments. With the dice so heavily loaded in favour of those with economic power, the policy response has been heavily influenced by a climate of inertia – that little can be done that strays too far outside the orthodox centre ground.[1]

Yet the market model of capitalism needs to be rolled back, reformed in a way that makes it work for all of society. This process might have started during the Blair/Brown era, but the entrenched model of corporate capitalism was preserved largely intact, with the state picking up much of the tab for its mounting social failures. Since 2010, that model has, if anything, become further entrenched, while the state's protective role has been greatly weakened, both trends creating the conditions for an ongoing hike in inequality.

The inadequacies of this model are now being seriously questioned beyond its traditional critics. The experiment in market fundamentalism is now widely discredited. The present economic system, with its inbuilt bias towards inequality and upward personal enrichment, is unsustainable. It has failed to deliver on its promises of faster growth and higher productivity, while creating the conditions for greater instability.

There are varied routes to reform, though few of them are firmly on the political agenda. This book sets out one possible set of measures that could form a part of this increasingly vital process of change. There is some evidence that, with more and more establishment figures calling for a new model of capitalism, the tide is turning, that the current bias towards inertia may be coming to an end. Social wealth funds and a citizen's income should be an essential part of this new tide of change.

Notes

Preface

[1] Mason, P., 'Airbnb and Uber's sharing economy', *The Guardian*, 21 June, 2015, www.theguardian.com/commentisfree/2015/jun/21/airbnb-uber-sharing-economy-dotcommunism-economy

Chapter 1

[1] Hopkins, P., 2015, 'We are warriors for the dispossessed', 13 March, www.conservativehome.com/thetorydiary/2015/03/we-are-warriors-for-the-dispossessed-goves-rallying-cry-for-the-conservatives.html

[2] www.bbc.co.uk/news/uk-politics-34460822

[3] Bourguignon, F., 2015, *The Globalization of Inequality*, Princeton: Princeton University Press, Chapter 2

[4] OECD, 2015, *In It Together: Why Less Inequality Benefits All*, Paris: OECD

[5] Piketty, T., 2014, *Capital in the twenty-first century*, Cambridge, MA: Harvard University Press, 'Introduction'

[6] *Observer*, 26 July 2015

[7] Carney, M., 2014, 'Inclusive capitalism: creating a sense of the systemic`, 27 May, www.financialstabilityboard.org/wp-content/uploads/Carney-Inclusive-Capitalism-Creating-a-sense-of-the-systemic.pdf

[8] OECD, 2014, *Shifting gear, policy challenges for the next fifty years*, OECD Policy Note No 24

[9] Lansley, S., 2011, *The Cost of Inequality*, London: Gibson Square, Chapter 3

[10] Ricardo, D., 1821, *The principles of taxation and political economy*, London: John Murray

[11] This is in some ways less the case in countries with a significant dependency on exports and investment for demand and growth. It would also be less of a problem if any shortfall of demand could be replaced by higher exports or investment, but this has not occurred in the UK during the wage squeeze from the early 1980s.

[12] Lansley, S. and Reed, H., 2013, 'How to boost the wage share', *TUC Touchstone Report*, London: TUC

[13] Ostry, J.D., Berg A. and Tsangarides, C.G., 2014, 'Redistribution, inequality and growth', *IMF Discussion Paper*, Washington: IMF

[14] OECD, 2014, 'Inequality hurts economic growth', 9 December, www.oecd.org/newsroom/inequality-hurts-economic-growth.htm See also: www.oecd-ilibrary.org/social-issues-migration-health/trends-in-income-inequality-and-its-impact-on-economic-growth_5jxrjncwxv6j-en

[15] ILO, 2014, 'Reducing inequality will boost economic growth', 24 January, www.ilo.org/global/about-the-ilo/newsroom/comment-analysis/WCMS_234482/lang--en/index.htm

[16] Dolphin, T., 2015, *The Missing Pieces: Solving the UK's Productivity Puzzle*, London: IPPR, Figure 5.2

Chapter Two

[1] Christiansen, H., 2011, *The Size and Composition of SOE in OECD countries*, Paris: OECD

[2] Mayo, E. (ed.), 2015, 'Co-operative Advantage: Why sharing business ownership is good for Britain', *New Internationalist*; see also Wilkinson, R. and Pickett, K., 2013, *A Convenient Truth*, London: Fabian Society

[3] Cass Business School, 2010, 'Employee-owned businesses', Summer, www.cassknowledge.com/inbusiness/feature/employee-owned-businesses; ILO, 2013, *Resilience in a Downturn* Geneva, ILO

[4] Christiansen, H., 2011, *The Size and Composition of SOE in OECD countries*, Paris: OECD

[5] Mahajan, S., 2006, 'Concentration ratios for businesses by industry in 2004', *Economic Trends*, 635, ONS, October

[6] Martin, S, 2015, 'World's top 100 companies worth £14.7tn', 2 June, www.ibtimes.co.uk/worlds-top-100-companies-worth-14-7tn-have-doubled-value-since-2009-pwc-report-1503963

[7] Bird, M., 2013, 'Global Britain', 28 September, www.cityam.com/article/1380157581/global-britain

[8] http://news.bbc.co.uk/1/hi/business/8482601.stm

[9] Sayer, A., 2014, *Why We Can't Afford the Rich*, Bristol: Policy Press, 94

[10] Sayer, A., 2014, *Why We Can't Afford the Rich*, Bristol: Policy Press, 93

NOTES

[11] Hutton, W., 2015, *How Good We Can Be*, London: Little Brown

[12] Marquand, D., 2014, *Mammon's Kingdom*, London: Penguin, Chapter 7

[13] Office for National Statistics, 2009, *Wealth in Great Britain: Main results from the wealth and assets survey 2006/08*, London: ONS. Moreover, the official data is known to understate the full extent of wealth concentration because of the frequency with which wealth holdings at the top are hidden.

[14] Hills, J., 2015, *Good Times Bad Times*, Bristol: Policy Press, 42-3

[15] Lansley, S. and Mack, J., 2015, *Breadline Britain, The Rise of Mass Poverty*, London: Oneworld, Chapter 7

[16] Speech by Andrew Haldane, 2015, 'Who owns a company?`, 22 May, www.bankofengland.co.uk/publications/Documents/speeches/2015/speech833.pdf

[17] Monaghan, A and Butler, S., 2014, 'Small businesses face "bullying" by corporate customers`, 11 December, www.theguardian.com/business/2014/dec/11/small-businesses-facing-bullying-corporate-customers

[18] Sikka, P., 2015, 'Corporate tax cuts help big business and small firms pay the price`, 7 April, https://theconversation.com/corporate-tax-cuts-help-big-business-and-small-firms-pay-the-price-39828

[19] Sembhy, R., 2015, 'Revealed: worst places to shop in Britain`, 21 May, www.ibtimes.co.uk/revealed-worst-places-shop-britain-why-topshops-philip-green-going-be-furious-1502349

[20] Brignall, M., 2015, 'It's rip-off Britain for broadband', *The Guardian*, 19 September

[21] Akerlof, G. and Shiller, R., 2015, *Phishing for Phools,* Princeton: Princeton University Press

[22] Oakly, D., 2015, 'Average FTSE 100 boss paid 150 times more than the average worker', *Financial Times*, 12 June

[23] *Daily Mail Comment*, 17 August 2015

[24] Smith, A., 1976, *An Inquiry into the Nature and Causes of the Wealth of Nations*, R.H. Campbell and A.S. Skinner (eds), Clarendon Press, I, II.iv.15, 357

[25] McElvee, S., 2014, 'On income inequality: an interview with Brank Milanovic', 14 November, www.demos.org/blog/11/14/14/income-inequality-interview-branko-milanovic

[26] Lansley, S. and Reed, H., 2013, 'How to boost the wage share', *TUC Touchstone Report*, London: TUC

[27] Weldon, D., 2015, 'Shareholder power holding back growth`, 24 July, www.bbc.co.uk/news/business-33660426

[28] See, for example, Wigglesworth, R. and Moore, E., 2015, 'Debt Markets: After the Binge', *Financial Times*, 5 August

29 Citizens Advice, 2015, 'Bogus self-employment costing millions to workers and government', 19 August, www.citizensadvice.org.uk/about-us/how-citizens-advice-works/media/press-releases/bogus-self-employment-costing-millions-to-workers-and-government/

30 Wilks-Heeg, S., Blick A. and Crone, S., 2012, *How Democratic is the UK? The 2012 Audit*, 31

31 Farnsworth, K., 2015, 'Britain's corporate welfare is out of control', *The Guardian*, 10 July, www.theguardian.com/commentisfree/2015/jul/10/corporate-welfare-budget-tax-money

32 Farnsworth, K., 2015, 'Britain's corporate welfare is out of control', *The Guardian*, 10 July

33 Lynne, M., 2015, 'It's not just the banks – our companies are also "too big to fail"', *Money Week*, 10 October

34 Martin, B., 2014, 'FTSE 100 companies hoard £53.5bn in cash', *Daily Telegraph*, 6 October

35 Carmichael, K., 2012, 'Free up "dead money" Carney exhorts corporate Canada, 22 August, www.theglobeandmail.com/report-on-business/economy/free-up-dead-money-carney-exhorts-corporate-canada/article4493091

36 Speech by Andrew Haldane, 2015, 'Who owns a company?`, 22 May, www.bankofengland.co.uk/publications/Documents/speeches/2015/speech833.pdf

37 Speech by Andrew Haldane, 2015, 'Who owns a company?`, 22 May, www.bankofengland.co.uk/publications/Documents/speeches/2015/speech833.pdf

38 Montgomerie, T., 2015, *What the world thinks of capitalism*, London: Legatum Institute; https://social.shorthand.com/montie/3C6iES9yjf/what-the-world-thinks-of-capitalism

39 Lent, A., 2015, *Small is Powerful*, Policy Network, 26 November; www.policy-network.net/pno_detail.aspx?ID=5019&title=Small-is-powerful-The-search-for-economic-equality-in-a-world-without-big-institutional-allies

40 Fink .L, 'BlackRock CEO tells the world's biggest business leaders to stop worrying about short-term results', 14 April, 2015, www.businessinsider.com/larry-fink-letter-to-ceos-2015-4?IR=T

41 Montgomerie, T., 2015, 'Capitalism's most dangerous enemies are on the right', *The Spectator*, 22 August

42 www.inc-cap.com/conference/conference-2015/general/#sthash.MLB697Y4.dpuf

43 Speech by Carney, M., 2014, 'Inclusive Capitalism: Creating a sense of the systemic', London, 27 May

44 Milanovic, B., 2015, 'Stiglitz: Theories of just deserts and exploitation`, 3 January, http://glineq.blogspot.co.uk/2015/01/stiglitz-theories-of-just-deserts-and.html

45 Lansley, S. and Reed, H., 2013, 'How to boost the wage share', *TUC Touchstone Report*, London: TUC

46 Prabhakar, R., Rowlingson, K. and White, S., 2008, *How To Defend Inheritance Tax*, London: Fabian Society

47 Piketty, T., 2014, *Capital in the twenty-first century*, Cambridge, MA: Harvard University Press, Chapter 15

48 Piketty, T., 2014, *Capital in the twenty-first century*, Cambridge, MA: Harvard University Press, Chapter 16, 569

49 Competition and Markets Authority, 2015, *Energy Market Investigation*, July

50 Meek, J., 2014, *Private Island: Why Britain Now Belongs to Someone Else*, London: Verso

Chapter Three

1 Association of Charitable Foundations, 2015, 'Giving Trends'. www.acf.org.uk/downloads/publications/Foundation_Giving_Trends_2015.pdf

2 Atkinson, A.B., 2015, *Inequality: What Can be Done?*, Harvard: Harvard University Press, 172–174

3 Published in Paine, T., 2005, *Common Sense and Other Writings*, NY: Barnes and Noble

4 Barnes, P., 2014, *With Liberty and Dividends for All*, Berrett-Koehler Publishers

5 Hayek, F.A., 2011, *The Constitution of Liberty: The Definitive Edition (Collected Works of F.A. Hayek)*, Chicago: University of Chicago Press

6 Cahill, K., 2012, *Who Owns Britain*, London: Canongate, 56

7 Riley, D., 2001, *Taken for a Ride: Taxpayers, Trains and HM Treasury*, Teddington: Centre for Land Policy Studies

8 Kay, R., 2014, 'Tech valuations bloat the entire economy', *Forbes*, 22 April

9 Cahill, K., 2012, *Who Owns Britain*, London: Canongate, 54

10 Barker, K., 2004, *Review of Housing Supply*, HMSO

11 Muellbauer, J., 2014, 'Six fiscal reforms for the UK's "lost generation"', 25 March, www.voxeu.org/article/six-fiscal-reforms-uk-s-lost-generation

12 Quoted in Seely, A., 2014, *Land Value Tax*, House of Commons Library Report

13 Institute for Fiscal Studies, 2011, *Tax by Design: the Mirrlees Review*, London: Institute for Fiscal Studies, Chapter 16

14 Letter to the *Guardian*, 12 October 2015

[15] For these constraints, see http://researchbriefings.files.parliament.uk/documents/SN06558/SN06558.pdf

[16] Makwana, R., 2015, 'From basic income to social dividend: sharing the value of common resource', *Share the World's Resources*, 18 March

[17] Lansley, S., 2011, *The Cost of Inequality*, London: Oneworld, Chapter 4

Chapter Four

[1] http://tea.texas.gov/index4.aspx?id=2147485578&menu_id=2147483695. See also: Nicolas, M., Firzli, J. and Franzel, J., 2014, 'Non-Federal Sovereign Wealth Funds in the United States and Canada', *Revue Analyse Financière*, Q3

[2] http://tea.texas.gov/index4.aspx?id=2147485578&menu_id=2147483695

[3] www.swfinstitute.org/sovereign-wealth-fund-rankings/

[4] Shields, J., 2013, 'Sovereign Wealth Funds' in Allen R, Hemming R and Potter, B, *The International Handbook of Public Financial Management*, London, Palgrave Macmillan

[5] The International Working Group for Sovereign Wealth Funds, 2008, 'The Santiago Principles`, October, www.iwg-swf.org/pubs/eng/santiagoprinciples.pdf

[6] PricewaterhouseCoopers, 2015, 'The role of sovereign investors in the global economy', July, www.pwc.com/gx/en/sovereign-wealth-investment-funds/publications/assets/major-role-of-sovereign-investors-in-the-global-economy.pdf

[7] Quoted in Wedmore, C., 2013, *Funding The Future: How Sovereign Wealth Funds benefit future generations*, London, Intergenerational Foundation

[8] Quoted in Ashton, J., 2015, 'How Abu Dhabi's mega-rich are buying up London', *Evening Standard*, 16 April

[9] Wedmore, C., 2013, *Funding The Future: How Sovereign Wealth Funds benefit future generations*, London: Intergenerational Foundation

[10] Hilton, A., 2015, 'Britain's trade deficit is a disaster waiting to happen', *Evening Standard*, 3 November

[11] Weiner, E.J., 2011, *The Shadow Market*, London: Oneworld, 1-3

[12] Cummine, A., 2013, 'Sovereign Wealth Funds: Can They Be Community Funds?', *Open Democracy*, 6 November

[13] Bagnall, A. and Truman, E., 2013, *Progress on Sovereign Wealth Fund Transparency and Accountability*, Peterson Institute for International Economics

[14] Cummine, A., 2013, 'Sovereign Wealth Funds: Can They Be Community Funds?', *Open Democracy*, 6 November

[15] Weiner, E.J., 2011, *The Shadow Market*, London: Oneworld, 205

[16] Quoted in Vander Weyer, M., 'Why hasn't Britain got a sovereign wealth fund?' *The Spectator*, 2 April 2008

[17] Quoted in Chakrobortty, A., 2014, 'Dude: Where's My North Sea Oil Money', *Guardian*, 13 June

[18] Atkinson, A.B., 2015, *Inequality, What Can Be Done?* Cambridge, MA, Harvard University Press, Chapter 6, 176–177

[19] Quoted in Centre for European Reform, 'State, money and rules: An EU policy for sovereign investment', December 2008, www.cer.org.uk/sites/default/files/publications/attachments/pdf/2011/essay_swf_dec08-1342.pdf

[20] Quoted in Cummine, A., 2015, 'A citizen's income and wealth fund for the UK: Lessons from Alaska', *Open Democracy*, 11 February

[21] Widerquist, K., 2013, 'The Alaska Model, A Citizen's Income in Practice', *Open Democracy*, 24 August.

[22] Widerquist, K., 2013, 'The Alaska Model, A Citizen's Income in Practice', *Open Democracy*, 24 August

[23] See, for example, Widerquist, K. and Howard, M.W. (eds), 2012, *Exporting the Alaska Model: Adapting the Permanent Fund Dividend for reform around the world*, Basingstoke: Palgrave Macmillan

[24] Heilbroner, R.L., 1980, 'The Swedish Promise', *New York Review of Books*, 4 December

[25] Interviewed on *Next Left*, Channel 4, February 1989; see also Meidner, R., 1978, *Employee Investment Funds*, London, Allen and Unwin.

[26] Blackburn, R., 2005 'Capital and Social Europe', *New Left Review*, 34, July

[27] Pontusson, J., 1992, *The Limits to Social Democracy: Investment Politics in Sweden*, Ithaca: Cornell University Press, 98

[28] Sassoon, D., 2013, *One Hundred Years of Socialism*, London: IB Taurus, 711

[29] Heilbroner, R.L., 1980, 'The Swedish Promise', *New York Review of Books*, 4 December

Chapter Five

[1] UK Financial Investments Ltd, 2014, *Annual Report and Accounts, 2013/14*, UK Financial Investments Ltd

[2] Department for Business, Innovation and Skills, 2015, *Apprenticeships Levy*, London: BIS, August

[3] www.gov.uk/government/speeches/chancellor-george-osbornes-summer-budget-2015-speech

[4] Murray, R. and Mulgan, G., 1993, *Reconnecting Taxation*, London: Demos, 23

[5] Detter, D. and Fölster, S., 2015, *The Public Wealth of Nations*, Basingstoke: Palgrave Macmillan

[6] Adonis, A., 2015, 'Why we should mobilise public land to tackle London's housing crisis', *CityAM*, 29 June

[7] www.publications.parliament.uk/pa/cm201516/cmselect/cmpubacc/289/28902.htm

[8] OECD, 2005, *Guidelines on Corporate Governance of State-owned Enterprises*, Paris: OECD

[9] Detter, D. and Fölster, S., 2015, *The Public Wealth of Nations*, Basingstoke: Palgrave Macmillan, 143

[10] Detter, D. and Fölster, S., 2015, *The Public Wealth of Nations*, Basingstoke: Palgrave Macmillan, 152

[11] Detter, D. and Fölster, S., 2014, 'Hidden Assets, How Countries Can Capitalize on Public Wealth', *Foreign Affairs*, 24 November

[12] Civil Society, 2015,'Why a raid on the Big Lottery Fund will blow up in he government's face`, 20 November, www.civilsociety.co.uk/finance/blogs/content/20800/bad_policy_even_worse_politics?topic=&print=1

[13] www.gov.uk/government/publications/summer-budget-2015/summer-budget-2015

[14] National Audit Office, 2015, *The Sale of Eurostar,* National Audit Office.

[15] Cumbers, A., 2014, *Renewing Public Ownership*, London: Centre for Labour and Social Studies, 7

[16] Allen, J. and Pryke, M., 2013 'Financialising household water', *Cambridge Journal of Regions, Economy and Society*, 6, 419-39

[17] Lobina, E. and Hall, D., 2013, *List of Water Remunicipalisations*, London: Public Services International Research Unit

[18] www.gov.uk/government/publications/summer-budget-2015/summer-budget-2015

[19] Muellbauer, J., 2015, 'Six fiscal reforms for the UK's "lost generation"', 25 March, www.voxeu.org/article/six-fiscal-reforms-uk-s-lost-generation

[20] Chennells, L., 1997, 'The Windfall Tax', *Fiscal Studies*, vol. 18, no. 3, pp. 279–291

[21] Seely, A., 2015, 'Taxation of Banking', *House of Commons Briefing Paper 05251*, September

[22] Holtham, G., 2014, 'Payment for Goods: Addressing the Social Democrat's Dilemma', *Juncture*, London: IPPR, 10 July; see also Holtham, G., 1995, 'A community fund could save social democracy', *The Independent*, 18 April

[23] Friedman M., 1969, *The Optimum Quantity of Money*, Piscataway, NJ, Transactions Publishers, 4

NOTES

[24] Turner A., 2015, *Between Debt and the Devil*, Princeton, Princeton University Press, Chapter 14, 220

[25] Holtham, G., 2014, 'Payment for Goods: Addressing the Social Democrat's Dilemma', *Juncture*, London: IPPR, 10 July

[26] Growth Business, 'UK M&A activity accounts for 45% of total European Value', 2 July 2015, www.growthbusiness.co.uk/news-and-market-deals/mergers-and-acquisitions/2488276/uk-manda-activity-accounts-for-45-of-total-european-value.thtml#sthash.RhSwGeL3.dpuf

[27] Corlett, A., Finch, D. and Whittaker, M., 2015, *Shape Shifting*, London: Resolution Foundation

[28] World Economic Forum, 2012, *Global Competitiveness Report, 2012-13* Geneva, World Economic Forum.

[29] Office for National Statistics, 2014, *UK Gross Domestic Expenditure on Research and Development, 2012*, London: ONS, March

[30] www.marxists.org/reference/archive/smith-adam/works/wealth-of-nations/book05/ch01c.htm

[31] Dolphin, T. and Nash, D., 2012, *Why We Need a State Investment Bank*, London: IPPR, 4

[32] Quoted in Harvey, F., 2015, 'Senior Tories slam government's Green Investment Bank sell-off', *The Guardian*, 25 June

[33] The Sutton Trust, 2009, *University Admissions Worldwide: A Percent Scheme for the UK?* London, The Sutton Trust.

[34] Care Quality Commission, 2015, *The state of health care and adult social care in England, 2014/1015*, London, CQC.

[35] Dilnot, A., 2011, *Commission on Funding of Care and Support*, London: Department of Health

[36] Hopkins, N. and Laurie, E., 2015, 'Using housing wealth to fund social care: why the Care Act 2014 is unfair', *British Politics and Policy blog*, London School of Economics

[37] Office for National Statistics, 2009, *Wealth in Great Britain: Main results from the wealth and assets survey 2006/08*, London: ONS

[38] Nicolles, N.,2015, 'Creative ways to address inequality in Europe`, 4 September, www.thersa.org/discover/publications-and-articles/rsa-blogs/2015/09/blog-creative-ways-to-address-inequality-in-europe/

[39] Barker, K., 2014, *Final Report of The Commission on the Future of Health and Social Care in England*, London: The King's Fund, 30-2

[40] Walker, K., 2015, Labour's Secret Plan', *Daily Mail*, 15 February

[41] Mulgan, G., 2015, 'Trotsky, Blair and the new Politics', *New Statesman*, 16 October

[42] Lawton, K. and Reed, H., 2013, *Property and Wealth Taxes in the UK*, London: IPPR, Chapter 1

43 Collinson, P., 2015, 'Inheritance tax was not designed for the super-rich – that's a Tory myth', *The Guardian*, 25 April

Chapter Six

1 Meade, J., 1964, *Efficiency, Equality and the Ownership of Property*, London: Allen and Unwin, 75

2 Lansley, S. and Reed, H., 2013, 'How to Boost the Wage Share', *TUC Touchstone Pamphlet*, London: TUC

3 Brynjolfsson, E. and Mcafee, A., 2014, *The Second Machine Age*, NY: W.W. Norton & Company; Ford, M., 2015, *The Rise of the Robots*, London: Oneworld

4 Kaplin, J., 2015, *Humans Need Not Apply*, Yale: Yale University Press

5 Cowen, T., 2013, *Average is Over*, NY: EP Dutton & Co Inc

6 Ford, M., 2015, *The Rise of the Robots*, London: Oneworld, 214

7 The levels of taxation required to reduce the after-tax return on capital to the rate of economic growth – a necessary condition for preventing ever-increasing wealth inequality – would be very high.

8 Meade, J., 1964, *Efficiency, Equality and the Ownership of Property*, London: Allen and Unwin, 66. See also White, S., 2013, 'Citizen ownership: the lost radicalism of the centre', *Open Democracy*, 8 November

9 White, S., 2009, 'Revolutionary liberalism? The philosophy and politics or ownership in the post-war Liberal Party', *British Politics*, 4, 2, 179

10 White, S., 2013 'Citizen ownership: the lost radicalism of the centre?', *Open Democracy*, 8, November; Jackson, B., (2005), 'Revisionism reconsidered: 'Property-owning democracy' and egalitarian strategy in post-war Britain', *Twentieth Century British History*, 16, 4, 416-440

11 The Labour Party, 1973, *Capital and Equality*, Opposition Green Paper, 9

12 The Labour Party, 1973, *Capital and Equality*, Opposition Green Paper, 31

13 SDP Working Party on Share Ownership, 1985, *Wider Share Ownership*

14 White, S., 2013, 'Citizen ownership: the lost radicalism of the centre', *Open Democracy*, 8 November

15 Ashdown, P., 1989, *Citizens' Britain: A Radical Agenda for the 1990s*, London: Fourth Estate, 129-30

16 Ashdown, P., 1989, *Citizens' Britain: A Radical Agenda for the 1990s*, London: Fourth Estate, 129-30

17 www.worker-participation.eu/National-Industrial-Relations/Countries/United-Kingdom/Financial-Participation/Basic-Data-on-Profit-Sharing-Employee-Share-Ownership; Tyson, L., 2015, 'The profit-sharing economy`, 31 July, www.project-syndicate.org/commentary/profit-sharing-economy-by-laura-tyson-2015-07

[18] Dumas, C., 2015, 'They've Broken the Bargain', *Prospect*, February

[19] High Pay Centre, 2014, *Reform Agenda: How to make top pay fairer*

[20] Haldane, A., 2015, 'Who owns a company', 22 May, www.bankofengland. co.uk/publications/Documents/speeches/2015/speech833.pdf

[21] Lansley, S., 2011, *The Cost of Inequality*, London: Gibson Square, Chapter 6

[22] www.bankofengland.co.uk/publications/Documents/quarterlybulletin/ qb120306.pdf

[23] Croucher, S., 2014, 'Bank of England QE a Robin Hood Tax in Reverse', *International Business Times*, 2 May

[24] www.ons.gov.uk/ons/rel/pnfc1/share-ownership---share-register-survey-report/2012/stb-share-ownership-2012.html

[25] Published in Paine, T., 2005, *Common Sense and Other Writings*, NY: Barnes and Noble

[26] White, S., 2013, 'Towards a Citizens' Inheritance', *Oxpol*, 16 December

[27] See, for example: Sandford, C., 1971, *Taxing Personal Wealth*, London: George Allen and Unwin; Nissan, D. and Le Grand, J., 2000, *A Capital Idea*, London: Fabian Society; White, S., 2013, 'Towards a Citizens' Inheritance', *Oxpol*, 16 December; Atkinson, A.B., 2015, *Inequality*, Harvard: Harvard University Press, p169-172, chapter 6. 169-72

[28] Sherradon, M., 1991, *Assets and the Poor*, NY: ME Sharpe Inc

[29] www.ucl.ac.uk/impact/case-study-repository/child-trust-fund

[30] Ben-Galim, D., 2011, *Asset Stripping, Child Trust Funds*, London: IPPR

Chapter Seven

[1] Russell, B., 2008, *Proposed Roads to Freedom: Socialism, Anarchism and Syndicalism*, ARC Manor

[2] Drucker, P., 1950, *The New Society: The Anatomy of Industrial Order*, London: William Heinemann Ltd

[3] Hayek, F.A., 1979, *Law, Legislation and Liberty, Vol 3: The Political Order of a Free People*, Chicago: University of Chicago Press, 54-5

[4] Friedman, M. and Friedman, R., 1990, *Free to Choose*, Thomson Learning; 1st Harvest

[5] Browne, J. and Hood, A., 2012, 'A Survey of the UK Benefit System', *IFS Briefing Note BN13*, London: IFS

[6] Browne, J. and Hood, A., 2012, 'A Survey of the UK Benefit System', *IFS Briefing Note BN13*, London: IFS, 60

[7] Torry, M., 2015, 'Two feasible ways to implement a revenue neutral CI scheme', *Euromod Working Papers EM 6/15*, Colchester: University of Essex.

[8] Gibb, J., 2015, 'How close is the new state Single Tier Pension to a Citizen's Pension?', *Citizen's Income Newsletter*, issue 2

[9] Makwana, R., 2015, 'Rethinking basic income in a sharing society', *Open Democracy*, 6 April

[10] Van Parijs, P., 1991, 'Why Surfers Should be Fed: The Liberal Case for an Unconditional Basic Income', *Philosophy & Public Affairs*, 20, 2, Spring, 101-31

[11] Rifkin, J., 1997, *The End of Work,* NY: Jeremy P Tarcher/Putnam

[12] Ford, M., 2015, *The Rise of the Robots*, London: Oneworld , p 256, Chapter 10.

[13] Standing, G., 2011, *The Precariat*, London: Bloomsbury

[14] See, for example, Torry, M., 2015, *101 Reasons for a Citizen's Income*, Bristol: Policy Press, 112

[15] Leonard, A., 2015, 'Rise of the Robots', *Los Angeles Times*, 21 May

[16] Solow, R., 2010, 'Whose Grandchildren', in L. Pecchi and G. Piga (eds), *Revisiting Keynes*, Cambridge, MA: MIT Press, 92

[17] Christensen, J., 2009, *Basic Income, social justice and freedom. Report from a symposium on themes from the work of Philippe Van Parijs*, University of York, Joseph Rowntree Foundation

[18] Levine R.A., Watts H., Hollister R., Williams W., O'Connor A., and Widerquist K., 'A Retrospective on the Negative Income Tax Experiments: Looking Back at the Most Innovative Field Studies in Social Policy', in Widerquist K., Lewis M. A., and Pressman S., eds), 2005, *The Ethics and Economics of the Basic Income Guarantee*, Farnham: Ashgate Publishing; 'Improving Social Security in Canada, Guaranteed Annual Income: A Supplementary Paper', Government of Canada, 1994

[19] See, for example, Standing, G., 2013, 'The poor are responsible too,' *The Financial Express*, 6 June, www.financialexpress.com/news/column-the-poor-are-responsible-too/1125548/0

[20] Standing, G., 2013, 'India's experiment in basic income grants', *Global Dialogue*, 3, 5, 24-6

[21] New Economics Foundation, 2015, *People, planet, power: towards a new social settlement*, February

[22] Huws, U., 2015, 'An Unconditional Citizen's Income', *Citizen's Income Newsletter*, issue 2

[23] Working Tax Credit, which is means-tested, is a dynamic subsidy. That is, it increases as wages fall. A citizen's income is a static subsidy, and does not increase as wages fall. Static subsidies have less of a wage-depressing effect than dynamic ones.

[24] Torry, M., 2015, 'Two feasible ways to implement a revenue neutral CI scheme', *Euromod Working Papers EM 6/15*, Colchester: University of Essex. See also Torry, M., 2014, 'Research Note: A feasible way to implement a Citizen's Income', *Institute of Social and Economic Research Working Paper,*

EM17/14, Colchester: University of Essex; *Citizen's Income Newsletter*, issue 1, 2015, 4-9

[25] Hirsch, D., 2015, *Could a Citizen's Income Work?*, York: Joseph Rowntree Foundation, 5-6; Reed, H. and Lansley, S., 2015, *The first results from a citizen's income simulation*, mimeo, Compass, December

[26] Hirsch, D., 2015, *Could a Citizen's Income Work?*, York: Joseph Rowntree Foundation, 5-6

[27] Torry, M., 2015, 'Two feasible ways to implement a revenue neutral CI scheme', *Euromod Working Papers EM 6/15*, Colchester: University of Essex.; and Reed, H. and Lansley, S., 2015, *The first results from a citizen's income simulation*, mimeo, Compass, December

[28] Torry, M., 2015, 'Two feasible ways to implement a revenue neutral CI scheme', *Euromod Working Papers EM 6/15*, Colchester: University of Essex.

[29] Torry, M., 2015, 'Two feasible ways to implement a revenue neutral CI scheme', *Euromod Working Papers EM 6/15*, Colchester: University of Essex.

[30] Atkinson, A.B., *Inequality – what can be done?*, 2015, Cambridge, MA, Harvard University Press, Chapter 8, 219-22

Chapter Eight

[1] The Intergenerational Foundation, 2013, *Funding the Future*

[2] Yoshioka, M., 2015, 'On capital: transforming sovereign wealth funds into community funds', RSA Blog, Royal Society of Arts, 27 April

[3] Lawrence, M., 2015, *Definancialisation: The Democratic Reform of Finance,* London: IPPR, 34

[4] Johnson, B., 2014, 'A Citizens' Wealth Fund would create billions for investment', *Daily Telegraph*, 5 October

[5] Gerrard, B., 2015, 'New wave of support for UK sovereign wealth fund', *Financial Times*, 19 July

[6] Clark, S., 2015, 'UK wealth fund to target private equity', *Wall Street Journal*, 14 August

[7] FTSE Global Markets, *GMPF/LPFA join the growing infrastructure trail*, 22 January, 2015, www.gmpf.org.uk/documents/panels/2015/06032015/item14.pdf

[8] Berry, C., 2015, *Take the Long Road*, Sheffield: Sheffield Political Economy Research Institute,

[9] www.scotland.gov.uk/Publications/2009/07/28112701/0

[10] Inman P., 2015, 'Turn crown estate into sovereign wealth fund`, 30 September,www.theguardian.com/money/2013/sep/30/crown-estate-sovereign-weath-fund-labour

[11] Hodgson, R., 2014, 'Let's make shale a gift that keeps on giving', *Daily Telegraph*, 10 November

[12] www.bbc.co.uk/news/uk-england-29968603

[13] Goodman P., 2015, 'Reasons to be Tory', 6 May, www.conservativehome. com/thetorydiary/2015/05/reasons-to-be-tory-13-a-sovereign-wealth-fund-for-the-north-of-england.html

[14] Gerrard, B., 2015, 'New Wave of Support for UK Sovereign Wealth Fund', *Financial Times*, 19 July

[15] Gerrard, B., 2015, 'New Wave of Support for UK Sovereign Wealth Fund', *Financial Times*, 19 July

[16] www.newton.co.uk/global/press-releases/cambridge-university-newton-investment-management-announce-partnership-long-horizon-investing/

[17] www.newton.co.uk/global/press-releases/cambridge-university-newton-investment-management-announce-partnership-long-horizon-investing/

[18] Tabatabai, H., 2012, 'Iran's Citizen's Income Scheme and its Lessons', *Citizen's Income Newsletter*, Issue 2

[19] Tabatabai, H., 2011, 'The Basic Income Road to Reforming Iran's Price Subsidies,' *Basic Income Studies*, 6.1, 1-24; Widerquist, K. and Howard, M.W. (eds) 2012, *Exporting the Alaska Model: Adapting the Permanent Fund Dividend for reform around the world*, NY: Palgrave Macmillan

[20] 'Switzerland: Government reacts negatively to UBI proposal', Basic Income News, 29 August 2014

[21] Sitra, 2015,'Think tank: a field experiment is the best way to test basic income', 1 December, www.sitra.fi/en/news/future/think-tank-tank-field-experiment-best-way-test-basic-income

[22] Basic Income Earth Network, 2015,'Finland: more than half of new MPs support basic income', 25 August, www.basicincome.org/news/2015/04/half-finish-parliament-support-basic-income/

[23] Basic Income Earth Network, 2015, 'Video: experimenting with free money', 9 April, www.basicincome.org/news/2015/04/video-experimenteren-met-gratis-geld-experimenting-with-free-money/

[24] http://basisinkomen.nl/

[25] Basic Income Earth Network, 2015, '30 Dutch municipalities show interest in basic income', 8 July, www.basicincome.org/news/2015/07/dutch-municipalities-experiments/

[26] Jourdain, S., 2015, 'French Regional Council to Assess the Feasibility of a Basic Income Pilot', *Basic Income Earth Network*, 9 July

[27] Taylor M., 2015,'A small chance to think big', 10 June, www.thersa.org/discover/publications-and-articles/matthew-taylor-blog/2015/06/a-small-chance-to-think-big/

[28] Adam Smith Institute, 2015,'Reform tax credits with a negative income tax', 26 October, www.adamsmith.org/news/press-release-reform-tax-credits-with-a-negative-income-tax-says-new-report/

29 Liberal Democrat Voice, 2015, 'Universal basic income is the way forward', 19 December, www.libdemvoice.org/opinion-universal-basic-income-is-the-way-forward-for-the-liberal-democrats-43836.html

30 http://policy.greenparty.org.uk/ec.html#EC730

31 http://basicincome.org.uk/2014/03/march-4h-peoples-parliament/

32 Hirsch, D., 2015, *Could a Citizen's Income Work?*, York: Joseph Rowntree Foundation, p 3

Chapter Nine

1 Ali, T., 2015, *The Extreme Centre*, London: Verso

Index